Table of Contents

Introduction

Who This Book Is For

You can probably guess from the title that this book is about data structures and algorithms, written for high schoolers by a high schooler. At the time of this writing, I have just finished my junior year at Milpitas High School in Milpitas, CA.

This book is intended for those students who have a basic understanding of the Java programming language and have used data structures such as ArrayLists, LinkedLists, Stacks and Queues, but want to dive deeper into understanding how they work. It would also be preferable to have a basic understanding of Algebra since we'll be using a bit of math to analyze how fast an algorithm runs.

This book will introduce you to the concept of time complexity and evaluating the speed at which a piece of code runs.

The first data structures we cover will be ArrayLists and LinkedLists - two classes that are useful in storing data in a sequence.

We also discuss Stacks and Queues. Stacks are useful when you want to store elements and get them out in a last-in-first-out (LIFO) manner.

Queues, on the other hand, are useful when you want to get things out in the order that you put them in.

The final data structure we discuss is the Binary Search Tree (BST). We introduce you to a very basic implementation. If you've ever used Java's TreeMap, then you're using a type of BST called a Red-Black tree. It's obviously very advanced for this book, but I urge you to look into it as well as another type of BST called an AVL tree.

Finally, we will go over sorting algorithms, namely Merge Sort and Quick Sort. These are very fast sorting algorithms and are actually used in Java itself (e.g., `Arrays.sort()`).

To make the best use of this book, you should play around with the code examples and test them out! Create instances of the classes, test out their methods, see if you can make them faster, or add in your own functionality. The choice is yours!

Chapter 1
Introduction to Time Complexity and Big O

Suppose you were given a list of natural numbers in random order and asked to arrange them from smallest to largest. How would you do it?

Your first approach might be to look for the smallest number and to move it to the beginning. Then you would look for the second smallest and move that to the second position, and then third smallest to the third, and so on until you reach the end of the list. This algorithm is known as **selection sort**, called that because you are selecting the next element and putting it in its proper position.

Now suppose a scientist came along and wanted to benchmark how fast different sorting algorithms ran compared to each other. How? The scientist would monitor how many operations occur. To better understand, let's take a look at a possible implementation of the selection sort.

```java
public class SelectionSort {
    public static void selectionSort(int[] arr) {
        if(arr == null || arr.length < 2)
            return;

        int n = arr.length;
        for(int i = 0; i < n - 1; i++) {
            // Find the minimum element in the
unsorted part of the array
            int minIndex = i;
            for(int j = i + 1; j < n; j++) {
                if(arr[j] < arr[minIndex])
                    minIndex = j;
            }
            // Swap the minimum element with the
first element in the unsorted part of the array
            int temp = arr[i];
            arr[i] = arr[minIndex];
            arr[minIndex] = temp;
        }
    }
}
```

To figure out how much time this algorithm takes to run, or its *time complexity*, we can count how many operations are executed.

Suppose we want to sort this array: {99, 44, 27, 8, 377, 21}. In this example, the length n = 6.

In the first iteration of the outer loop, we loop over 5 elements—44, 27, 8, 377, 21—to find the minimum. This is basically n - 1 steps. In this first iteration, we find element 8 to be the minimum, so we swap it with the first element of the array:

In the second iteration of the outer loop, we loop over 4 elements—27, 99, 377, 21—to find the minimum. This is n - 2 steps. In this second iteration, we find element 21 to be the minimum, so we swap it with the second element of the array:

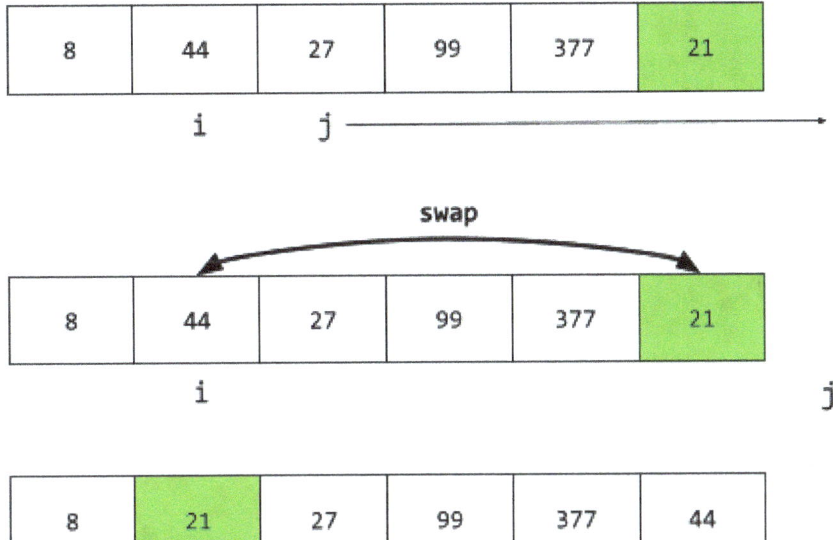

When the final iteration of the outer loop completes, we soon realize that there is a pattern: the total number of operations keeps decreasing by one. In this particular example, the total number of operations is 5 + 4 + 3 + 2 + 1. Thus, we can generalize the time complexity for selection sort to be:

$$(n - 1) + (n - 2) + \ \ldots\ + 1 = \frac{n(n-1)}{2} = \frac{1}{2}(n^2 - n)$$

When it comes to measuring time complexity, one interesting thing we need to be aware of is that constant terms are disregarded; we only focus on the dominant term that grows the fastest as n increases. In the case of

$$\frac{1}{2}(n^2 - n)$$

we disregard the ½ coefficient. We are left with

$$n^2 - n$$

We also eliminate the -n term because we only care about the n^2 term since it grows the fastest as n grows. We are left with

$$n^2$$

So the time complexity of the selection sort is $O(n^2)$, pronounced as "O of n squared". This is called "Big O Notation" and we use it to indicate the time complexity of an algorithm with respect to n, which is usually the length of the array, or the size of the input in general. Note that it will give you a rough estimate of how the program runs, not the exact time.

In general, Big O notation refers to how many steps it takes for a program to run. Thus, we can use Big O notation to compare the time complexity of different algorithms. For example, if one algorithm is $O(n^2)$ and another is $O(n)$, we know that the former will run much slower as n gets larger. Think about it—which would be faster: a program with 100 steps or 100^2 steps?

Let's take a look at another example. Instead of selection sort this time, we will use the **bubble sort** algorithm.

```java
public class BubbleSort {
    public static void bubbleSort(int[] arr) {
        if(arr == null || arr.length < 2)
            return;

        int n = arr.length;
        for(int i = 0; i < n - 1; i++) {
            for(int j = 0; j < n - i - 1; j++) {
                // If the current element is greater
than the next element, then swap them
                if(arr[j] > arr[j + 1]) {
                    int temp = arr[j];
                    // Imitates the highest element
bubbling up to the top
                    arr[j] = arr[j + 1];
                    arr[j + 1] = temp;
                }
            }
        }
    }
}
```

To understand the above code, imagine we had to sort a collection of different-sized blocks. In the first iteration of the outer loop, we analyze each pair. If the block on the left is taller than the one on the right, we swap. If not, we do nothing. We then proceed to the next pair and so on. When the first iteration of the outer loop completes, we can see that the tallest block has bubbled its way to the right.

Here's a visual depiction of that first iteration:

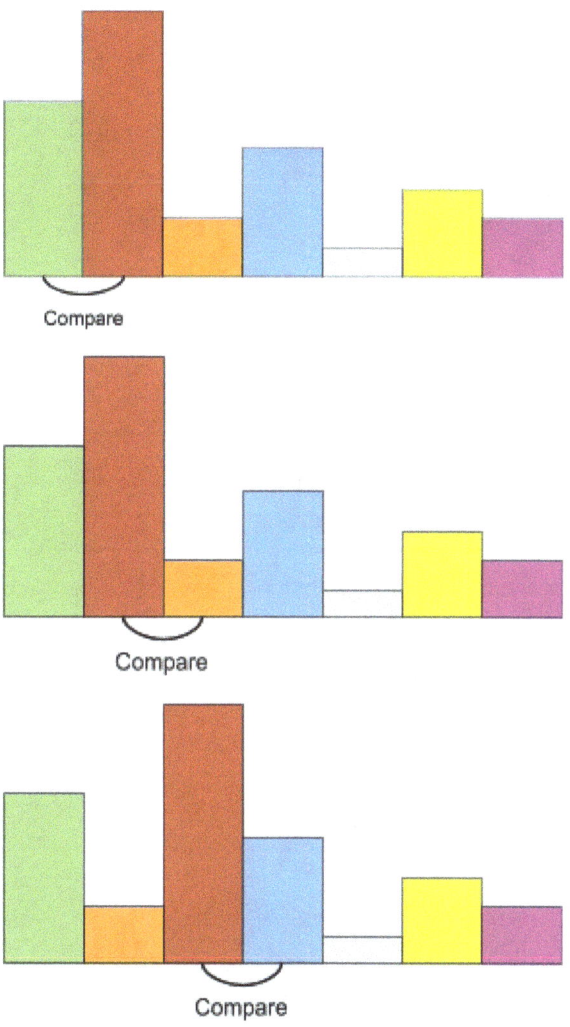

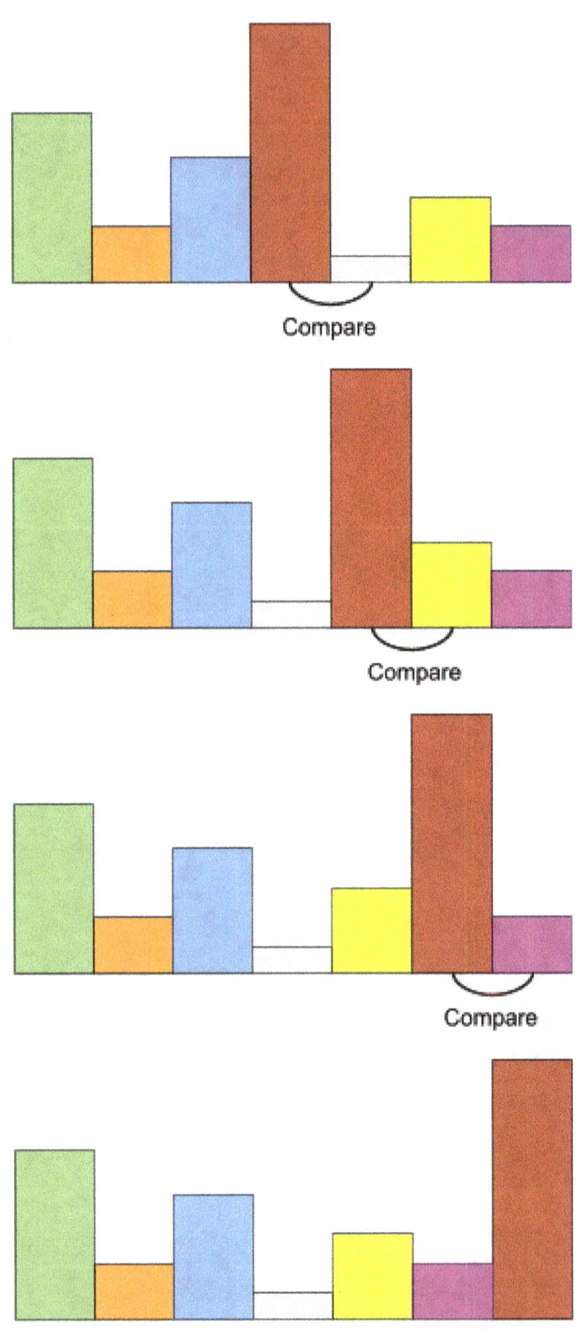
Compare
Compare
Compare

From the steps above, you can see that the tallest block–the red one–bubbles its way to the right. What do you think will happen in the next iteration? Well, from the logic in the code, the green block should bubble its way to the right and be placed right next to the red.

To analyze the time complexity of a bubble sort, we need to see how many operations are performed, just like in a selection sort. Each iteration of the outer loop has n – 1, n – 2, … 1 operations. Just like before, this means there are $\frac{1}{2}(n^2 - n)$ operations, which as we know is O(n²).

The most common time complexities you will come across are:

O(1)

Constant time - any algorithm that takes the same amount of time to run regardless of the input size. For example:

```java
public static void printLength(int[] arr) {
    System.out.println(arr.length);
}
```

The above code is O(1) because no matter how big the array is, there is only one operation to be carried out, so the runtime is constant. Also note that if there were more than one operation, the time complexity would still be O(1) as long as the number of operations doesn't depend on the size of the input (the length of the array). So printing three different things would still be O(1) because O(3) reduces to O(1) from our definition.

O(n)

Linear time - any algorithm that is linearly dependent on the size of the input. For example:

```java
public static int arraySum(int[] arr) {
    int sum = 0;
    for(int a : arr)
        sum += a;

    return sum;
}
```

The runtime of the code above increases linearly with the size of the input. If you added 3 elements to the array for example, the loop would iterate 3 more times, which is the same as going from n elements to n + 3. Again note that all constants are disregarded and only the highest term is kept, so O(2n), O(3n), and O(n + 10) are all equivalent to O(n).

O(n^2)

Quadratic time - this is common in algorithms like the ones we previously discussed where an outer loop and an inner loop both iterate through the entire array.

O(2^n) or O(k^n)

Exponential time - this often occurs in recursive methods that call themselves 2 times or k times, respectively. For example:

```java
public static int fibonacci(int n) {
    if(n <= 1)
        return n;

    return fibonacci(n-1) + fibonacci(n-2);
}

public static void main(String[] args) {
    for(int i = 0; i < 20; i++)
        System.out.println("fibonacci(" + i + ") = "
+ fibonacci(i));
}
```

The fibonacci method calls itself 2 times per method call. Thus, every method call will result in 2 more method calls branching off of that one, and since the time complexity grows exponentially as n increases, the time complexity is O(2^n). More generally, methods that call themselves k times in each call are usually O(k^n).

O(log n)

O(log n) usually means that the time complexity is $\log_2$ of n.

Imagine that you want to find the index of an element in an array that's already sorted. You might choose to loop through the entire array and stop once you reach that element, which is O(n) complexity since you iterate over the entire array. You can choose to do a **binary search**, which is a fast, O(log n) algorithm to find the index of an element in an array:

```java
public static int binarySearch(int[] arr, int target)
{
    int low = 0;
    int high = arr.length - 1;

    while(low <= high) {
        int mid = low + (high-low)/2;
        if(arr[mid] == target)
            return mid;
        else if(arr[mid] > target)
            high = mid - 1;
        else
            low = mid + 1;
    }

    return -1;
}
```

The algorithm works by taking a sorted array and comparing the middle element to the value you want to find. If the value is greater than the middle, then you search to the right to find bigger values in the array; otherwise, you search to the left. Each iteration reduces the search space by half, so there are $\log_2 n$ iterations, meaning the time complexity is $O(\log_2 n)$. For example, take the array size to be 16:

After 1 iteration, the search space would be 8.
After 2 iterations, the search space would be 4.
After 3 iterations, the search space would be 2.
After 4 iterations, you have (presumably) found the element.

Thus, it takes at most 4 iterations to find the element or to see that the element isn't within the array. This matches our expected time complexity since $\log_2 16 = 4$.

Binary search is faster than a regular linear search because with a linear search, you might have to scan the entire array to find a certain element, which takes n steps. With a binary search, you narrow down the search space by half every time, which is more efficient.

O(n log n)

Found in certain sorting algorithms, O(n log n) usually involves a method that recursively splits the array into two parts and then another method that runs some sort of comparison on each element of each part.

The splitting method is O(log n) since, like the binary search algorithm presented above, each splitting divides the space in half.

Then the comparison method runs, which involves iterating over each half. This results in the runtime for the method being O(n).

Thus, the entire algorithm would be O(n log n) because the splitting step occurs log n times, while the other step requires n comparisons.

One example of an O(n log n) algorithm would be **merge sort**. It works by recursively dividing the input array into halves until it reaches a point where each half is only one element. Then, it merges the halves back together in a sorted order. The time complexity of the merge operation is O(n), while the splitting is O(log n).

We will explore merge sort in more detail in Chapter 8. For now, just understand that algorithms like mergesort that divide up the array and perform a comparison on each and every element are usually of O(n log n) time complexity.

Below is a graph of the same common time complexities listed above and how they compare.

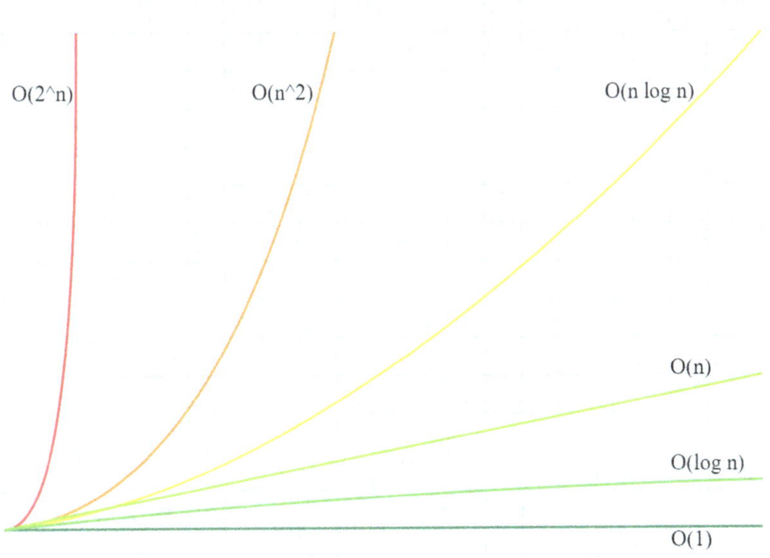

Note that these are very small values of n. The bottom 3 functions–O(1), O(log n), and O(n) respectively–will stay relatively small compared to the top 3.

O(n log n), O(n^2), and O(2^n) grow extremely fast, so you can see that as n gets bigger, the top 3 will get very high, very quickly. This means that programs with such time complexities will take much more time to run as the input size increases.

Chapter Summary

In this chapter, we learned about *time complexity* - a measure of how much time it takes an algorithm to run as the input size grows. To compare the time complexity of algorithms, we used Big O notation. The most common, listed from fastest to smallest, are $O(1)$, $O(\log n)$, $O(n)$, $O(n \log n)$, $O(n^2)$, and $O(2^n)$ or $O(k^n)$.

To illustrate this concept, we introduced several algorithms. The first two were sorting algorithms - selection sort and bubble sort. Since each ran in quadratic time (i.e., $O(n^2)$), they are said to have the same time complexity.

The other example was binary search. With every iteration of the search, the number of elements to search was reduced in half, thus making the time complexity of the algorithm to be $O(\log n)$.

Chapter 2

MyList

Suppose you want to write a program that stores the ages of your friends in a list. One way is to use an array of integers like this:

```java
int[] ages = new int[8];
ages[0] = 16;
ages[1] = 17;
ages[2] = 15;
...
ages[7] = 17;
```

From the above code, you can see that we're creating an array big enough to hold the ages of up to eight people. What if later on in the program you needed to add two more friends? As you already know, arrays in Java are fixed-sized objects - they do not expand/grow. To add more ages, one solution is to:

1. Create a new and bigger array (e.g., length of 16)
2. Copy the elements from the old array to the new one
3. Add the two new friends' ages to the new array

Wouldn't it be great if there was a data structure that we could use to store objects (e.g., integers representing ages) and not have the restriction that its size be fixed? In Java, there is such a thing: **java.util.List**. If you look carefully, you'll realize that List is really an interface; the actual implementations of List are in the **java.util.ArrayList** and **java.util.LinkedList** classes. They are dynamic data structures that can grow in size and can store elements of any type.

For the purposes of this book, we will create a very basic interface similar to Java's List. We'll call it **MyList**. From the code below, it's obvious that our interface has fewer methods. Moreover, it only works with integers instead of Objects or generics. The reason for such a simple interface is to illustrate the concepts of a particular data structure by focusing on its most important operations.

```java
public interface MyList {

    // Add data to the end of the list
    void add(int data);

    // Add data to the given position of the list
    void add(int index, int data);

    // Remove data from the given position
    void remove(int index);
```

```java
    // Replace data at the given position
    void set(int index, int data);

    int get(int index);
    int size();
}
```

As you can see from the method signatures above, any subclass of MyList must implement all six of the interface's methods.

The `add(int data)` method allows you to add data to the end of the list.

The `add(int index, int data)` method allows you to add data to a specific position in the list. For example, if you have a list with two elements and you want to add a third element to the middle, you would do something like this:

```java
// Add first element
myList.add(100); // myList: {100}

// Add second element
myList.add(200); // myList: {100,200}

// Add third element to middle of list
myList.add(1, 150); // myList: {100,150,200}
```

What happens when you try to add to a negative index? Or to an index larger than the list's size? In both cases, an **IndexOutOfBoundsException** will be thrown.

The `remove(int index)` method allows you to remove data at a specific position. Again, if you try to remove from an empty list, a negative index, or an index equal to or greater than the list's size, an IndexOutOfBoundsException will be thrown.

The `set(int index, int data)` method allows you to replace the data at the given position. If you try to replace from an empty list, a negative index, or an index equal to or greater than the list's size, an IndexOutOfBoundsException will be thrown.

The `get(int index)` method is used to retrieve the data that you previously stored at the given index. If you try to retrieve from an empty list, a negative index, or an index equal to or greater than the list's size, an IndexOutOfBoundsException will be thrown.

The `size()` method should be very straightforward as it retrieves the size of the list.

So, continuing with the example above, let's try out some of the other operations:

```java
// Set the second element to 151
```

```java
myList.set(1, 151); // myList: {100,151,200}

// Add 150 to the second position
myList.add(1, 150); // myList: {100,150,151,200}

// Remove the third element
myList.remove(2); // myList: {100,150,200}

// Loop and print
for(int i = 0; i < myList.size(); i++)
    System.out.println(myList.get(i));
```

Now that you've seen what MyList can do, let's go ahead and actually implement this simple interface. As you may recall, Java has its ArrayList and LinkedList. We will have something similar.

In Chapter 3, we will define a subclass called **MyArrayList** which is a data structure that uses an array under the hood. We will go into detail about how that backing array is used to support the operations of MyList.

In Chapter 4, we will define another subclass of MyList called **MyLinkedList**. Instead of using an array to store data, MyLinkedList uses nodes that are "linked" together to store values, hence the name.

Chapter Summary

In this chapter, we defined an interface–`MyList`–that is similar to `java.util.List`. Although it has fewer methods, the methods that `MyList` does have are very important for introducing the core concepts of the dynamic nature of a `List` implementation, namely the ability to grow. The next two chapters will cover such implementations.

Chapter 3
MyArrayList

In this chapter, we will define a class called
MyArrayList which implements the MyList interface
from Chapter 2.

As hinted in its name, MyArrayList uses an array to hold
its data. The class has an `INITIAL_SIZE` of eight.

So, let's begin with a barebones `MyArrayList`:

```java
public class MyArrayList implements MyList {

    private static final int INITIAL_SIZE = 8;

    private int[] arr = new int[INITIAL_SIZE];
    private int size;

    public int size() {
        return size;
    }
}
```

Don't worry that the code won't compile right now. We
will continue to add to the class. By the end of this
chapter, we should have a complete class that compiles
and runs!

The main takeaway from the above code is that
MyArrayList contains an array called `arr` that is
initialized with a length of eight.

`arr:`

0	1	2	3	4	5	6	7
0	0	0	0	0	0	0	0

Before we implement any more methods, we have to
make sure that elements that we try to add or modify
are within the bounds of the space that we are working
with. We implement this behavior in a method called
`checkIndex`:

```java
private void checkIndex(int index, boolean inclusive)
{
    if(inclusive && index == size)
        return;

    if(index < 0 || index >= size)
        throw new IndexOutOfBoundsException(index + "
is out of bounds.");
}
```

Looking at the code, you can see that it takes two
parameters—the index to be checked and whether the
check should be inclusive. If the check is inclusive, the

method will allow the index to be the same as the size. Otherwise, an exception is thrown if the index is negative or out of the bounds of the list.

Now that we have an array, let's implement the add methods.

Add

```java
// Add data to the end of the list
public void add(int data) {
    add(size, data);
}

public void add(int index, int data) {
    checkIndex(index, true);

    // Check if resizing is needed
    if(size == arr.length) {
        int[] newArr = new int[arr.length * 2];
        for(int i = 0; i < arr.length; i++)
            newArr[i] = arr[i];

        arr = newArr;
    }

    // Before writing, we need to shift every element
one index to the right starting from the end
    for(int i = size; i > index; i--)
        arr[i] = arr[i - 1];

    // Put data in the correct position
```

```
    arr[index] = data;
    size++;
}
```

That's a lot to digest, so let's take things one step at a
time.

The add(int data) method actually calls the add(int
index, int data) method and passes the size
variable. The size variable not only represents the
number of elements already in the list, it also represents
the end position to which new data will be inserted.

The add(int index, int data) method does most of
the work. It calls checkIndex() to make sure the index is
not out of bounds.

It also checks if the current array is big enough to hold
the new data. If not, a new array is instantiated with
double the current array's length. All values from the old
array are copied to the new array. The new array is now
used as the backing array of MyArrayList.

Lastly, our add method tries to make sure we don't
overwrite whatever element currently occupies the
position at index. It will shift the entire subarray starting
at index one step to the right. This frees up the slot at
index. Thus, the last step is to insert at that spot.

To illustrate the shifting, let's suppose we have an instance of `MyArrayList` with a size 6. The backing array would look something like this:

`arr:`

0	1	2	3	4	5	6	7
0	1	2	3	4	5		

Let's assume we want to insert the number 88 at index 1. To make room for the new element, we copy every element to the right, starting from index 1:

`arr:`

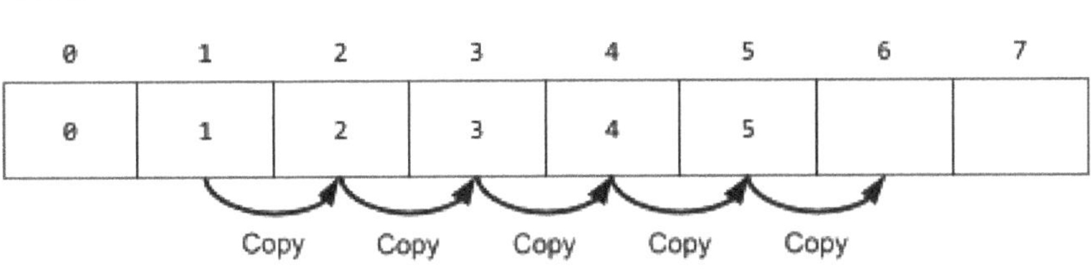

`arr (after copying):`

0	1	2	3	4	5	6	7
0	1	1	2	3	4	5	

Notice how every element starting from the insertion point has been shifted one position to the right. Once this shifting is done, the insertion can take place:

```
arr:
```

0	1	2	3	4	5	6	7
0	88	1	2	3	4	5	

After insertion, we increment the `size` variable.

Remove

Now that we know how to add an element to the list, we need to have a way to remove elements. The following is how this would work:

```java
public void remove(int index) {
    checkIndex(index, false);

    for(int i = index + 1; i < size; i++)
        arr[i - 1] = arr[i];

    arr[size--] = 0;
}
```

Again, the method starts by checking the index to make sure it is contained within the array. Then, in order to remove an element at that index, all elements after it are shifted one step to the left. We can demonstrate this with an example. Suppose we want to remove the element 88 (i.e., at index 1) from the following array:

arr:

0	1	2	3	4	5	6	7
0	88	1	2	3	4	5	

We start by copying every element to the left, starting from index 2:

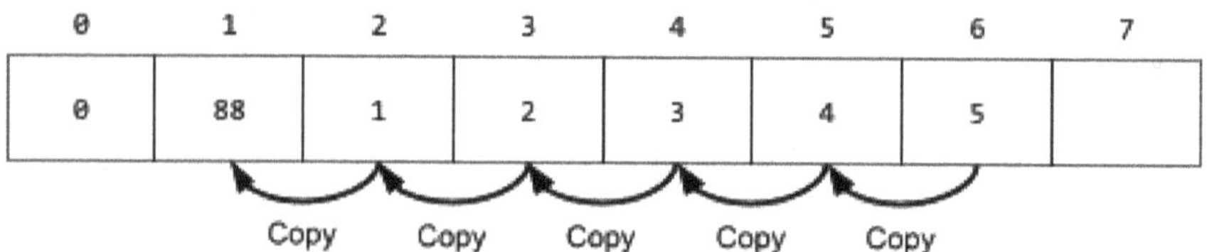

arr (after copying):

0	1	2	3	4	5	6	7
0	1	2	3	4	5	5	

Notice how every element starting from one position to the right of the deletion point has been shifted one position to the left. Once this shifting is done, all we need to do is decrement the `size` variable and optionally blank out the last element, which essentially makes the array like this:

arr:

0	1	2	3	4	5	6	7
0	1	2	3	4	5		

Get

To get a value from an index in the array, we only need to make sure that the index is within the bounds of the list. If it is, then we can return the value at that index.

```java
public int get(int index) {
    checkIndex(index, false);
    return arr[index];
}
```

Set

Similarly, to change a value at an index in the array, we need to ensure the index is within the bounds and then set the slot to its new value.

```java
public void set(int index, int data) {
    checkIndex(index, false);
    arr[index] = data;
}
```

Full Implementation

```java
public class MyArrayList implements MyList {

    private static final int INITIAL_SIZE = 8;

    private int[] arr = new int[INITIAL_SIZE];
    private int size;

    public int size() {
        return size;
    }

    private void checkIndex(int index, boolean inclusive) {
        if(inclusive && index == size)
```

```java
        return;

    if(index < 0 || index >= size)
        throw new IndexOutOfBoundsException(index
+ " is out of bounds.");
    }

    // Add data to the end of the list
    public void add(int data) {
        add(size, data);
    }

    public void add(int index, int data) {
        checkIndex(index, true);

        // Check if resizing is needed
        if(size == arr.length) {
            int[] newArr = new int[arr.length * 2];
            for(int i = 0; i < arr.length; i++)
                newArr[i] = arr[i];

            arr = newArr;
        }

        // Before writing, we need to shift every
element one index to the right starting from the end
        for(int i = size; i > index; i--)
            arr[i] = arr[i - 1];

        // Put data in the correct position
        arr[index] = data;
        size++;
    }
```

```java
    public void remove(int index) {
        checkIndex(index, false);

        for(int i = index + 1; i < size; i++)
            arr[i - 1] = arr[i];

        arr[size--] = 0;
    }

    public int get(int index) {
        checkIndex(index, false);
        return arr[index];
    }

    public void set(int index, int data) {
        checkIndex(index, false);
        arr[index] = data;
    }
}
```

Analysis of Time Complexities

size() - O(1) because only 1 operation is being performed - returning the size variable.

add(int data) - This is usually O(1) since there is only 1 operation being performed - changing a value of the array to a new one. However, when the array happens to be at the maximum size, then we need to resize the array to add more space for the new element. Thus, this method can be O(n) because resizing actually copies every element from the original array into a new array.

`add(int index, int data)` - Worst case is O(n) when you add to the beginning, causing every element to shift down one index to accommodate. Best case is O(1), adding to the end of the ArrayList without having to resize or shift.

`remove(int index)` - When an element is removed, every element after it must be shifted back one space in order to properly represent the new state of the array. When you remove at the beginning of the ArrayList, this method could take n steps. For the same reasons as above, this method is O(n) in the worst case and O(1) in the best.

`get(int index)` and `set(int index, int data)` - Both are O(1) since each method runs in constant time. `get()` returns one element and `set()` changes one element.

Use Cases

ArrayLists are useful when:
- You need a dynamic array that can grow
- You need to frequently access elements by index, since `get()` and `set()` run in O(1) time
- You don't require high performance for operations like insertion or removal at arbitrary positions since they can take O(n) time.

Chapter Summary

In this chapter, we created a concrete implementation of MyList: MyArrayList. Since it's a subclass of MyList, you can create instances of it like this:

```java
MyList myList = new MyArrayList();
```

You can then add items to it, or you can remove from it. And since it's a list, you can always be sure that it maintains a certain order (i.e., insertion order). But most importantly, it can grow dynamically. You can continue to add items to it without having to worry about resizing because it knows how to resize itself.

Chapter 4

MyLinkedList

Similar to an ArrayList, a LinkedList provides a way to store a sequence of elements. And since both are subclasses of the List interface, you can perform the same operations on a LinkedList as you would on an ArrayList. Thus, you can add or remove items, access individual items, and get the size of the list.

However, a LinkedList is different from an ArrayList in that instead of storing each element in an array, a LinkedList uses instances of a helper class called a `Node`.

LinkedLists get their name from the references between nodes, which form connections similar to a chain-link. Each node is linked to the node after it and the node before it, and each node also stores its corresponding data value. For example, suppose we had the list {1, 2, 3}:

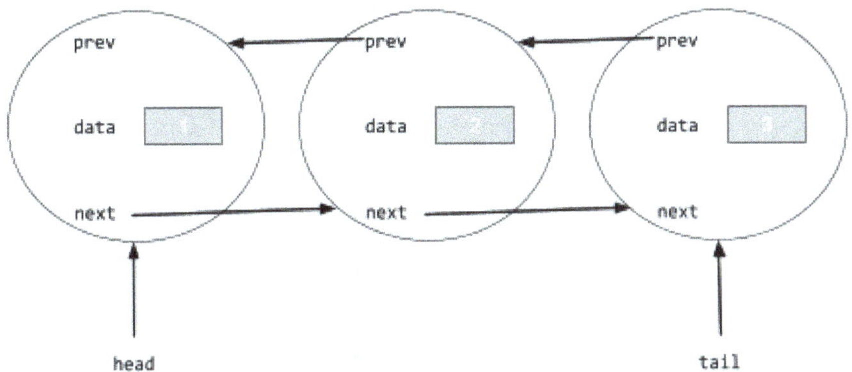

Note that **next** and **prev** are Node instance variables. prev points to the node that comes before the current node, or null if it is the first node. Likewise, next points to the node that comes after the current node, or null if the current node is at the end. Also, we call the first node the **head** and the last node the **tail**. If this is confusing, don't worry, it will make a lot more sense when you see the Java implementation.

In this chapter, we will create a class called **MyLinkedList** that represents a basic LinkedList. It will implement the interface MyList and will have a Node called head and a Node called tail, which represent the first and last Nodes in the LinkedList, respectively.

Here is the code for the Node class:

```java
private class Node {
    int data;
    Node prev;
    Node next;
```

```java
    public Node(int data) {
        this.data = data;
    }
}
```

You can see that each Node instance stores its element in the **data** attribute, along with a reference to the previous and next Nodes in the list.

Now we will begin our MyLinkedList class definition:

```java
public class MyLinkedList implements MyList {
    private Node head;
    private Node tail;
    private int size;

    private static class Node {
        int data;
        Node prev;
        Node next;

        public Node(int data) {
            this.data = data;
        }
    }

    private void checkIndex(int index, boolean
inclusive) {
        if(inclusive && index == size)
            return;

        if(index < 0 || index >= size)
            throw new IndexOutOfBoundsException(index
+ " is out of bounds.");
    }

    public int size() {
        return size;
    }
}
```

Again, our class will implement the MyList interface. We will borrow the `size()` and `checkIndex()` methods from the MyArrayList class that we wrote in the previous chapter. MyLinkedList also holds two `Node` references: one to the `head` and one to the `tail` of the list.

You may notice that the `Nodes` don't store their indices, and we currently have no way to get a `Node` at a certain index. Let's fix that with the following method:

```java
private Node getNode(int index) {
    Node curr;
    if(index < size / 2) {
        curr = head;
        for(int i = 0; i < index; i++)
            curr = curr.next;
    } else {
        curr = tail;
        for(int i = size - 1; i > index; i--)
            curr = curr.prev;
    }

    return curr;
}
```

The good thing about having the `Nodes` be doubly-linked (they have a reference to both the previous and next `Nodes`) is that you can find an index from both ends of the list. That means that you can start from either the `head` or the `tail` when searching for a `Node` at an index.

Why is this useful?

When a `Node` is located near the end of the list, instead
of starting at the beginning and searching through the
whole list, we can start at the `tail` and go backward
(through the `prev` pointers) to find that index. Similarly,
if the index is at the beginning, we can instead start
from the `head` and go forward, using the `next` pointers,
to find an index.

The method then starts from the appropriate side and
navigates through the `Nodes` until it finds the correct
index and returns that `Node`.

Add

Let's start with a basic add method:

```java
public void add(int data) {
    add(size, data);
}

public void add(int index, int data) {
    checkIndex(index, true);
    Node newNode = new Node(data);
    size++;
    // TODO: link newNode
}
```

Essentially, we have created a new `Node` and increased the `size`, but we need to figure out where to put `newNode` in the list.

There are 3 cases to consider when adding a `Node`. The first is when you are adding to the beginning of the list, i.e. `index = 0`.

If the `index` is 0, it means we want to have the new element be the `head`.

If the list is empty, all we need to do is assign both `head` and `tail` to the `newNode`:

```java
if(index == 0) {
    if(head == null)
        head = tail = newNode;
    else {
        // If list was not already empty
    }
}
```

If the `head` is not `null`, meaning the list is not empty, we need to link the `newNode` right before the current head. Here's how we will do it:

```java
head.prev = newNode;
newNode.next = head;
head = newNode;
```

First, we set the prev pointer of the current head to point
to the newNode and the newNode's next to the head in
order to maintain the doubly-linked nature of the list.
Then, the head variable is updated to point to the
newNode.

Let's illustrate this with an example. Suppose we have a
LinkedList containing 1, 2, and 3:

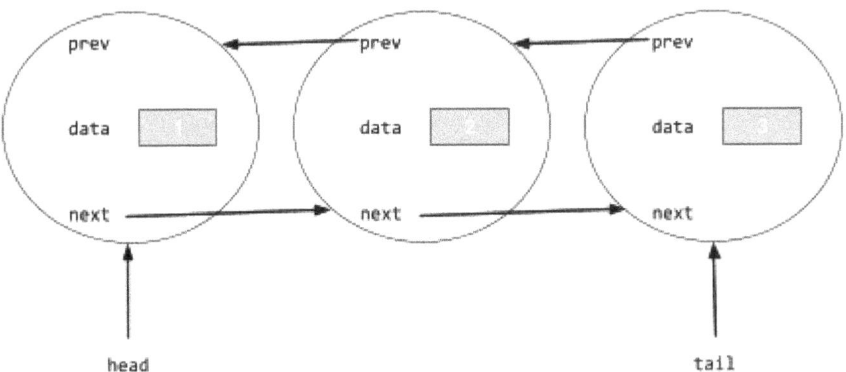

And we want to add 0 to the beginning of the list.
First, we create a new Node called newNode:

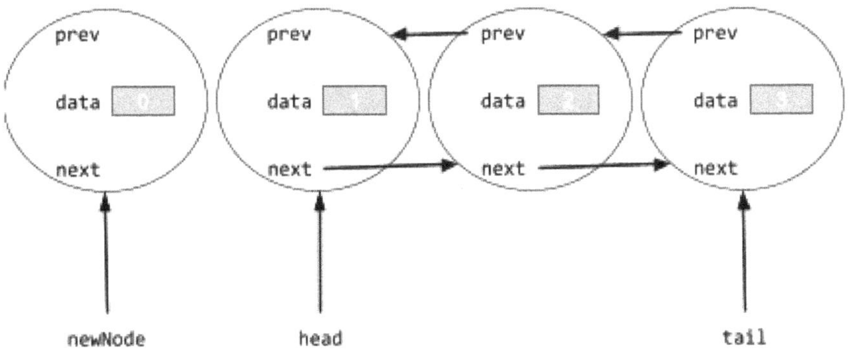

Then we set newNode's next pointer to point to the head:

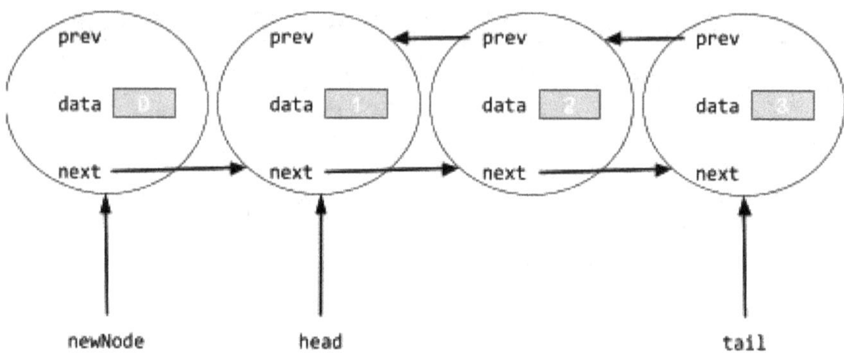

Then, we make the head's prev pointer point back to
newNode:

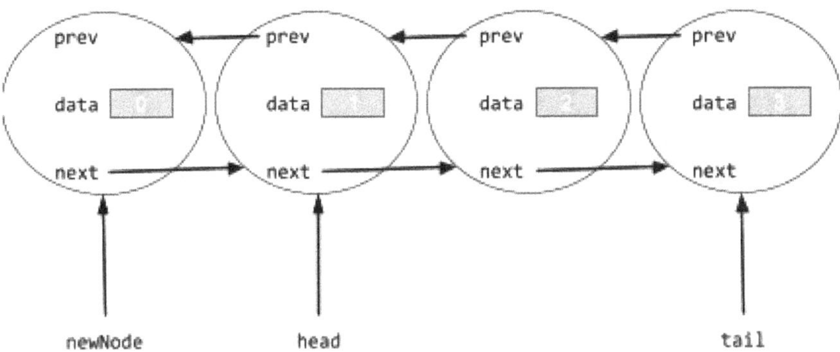

And finally, we need to fix the head so that It points to
the correct Node:

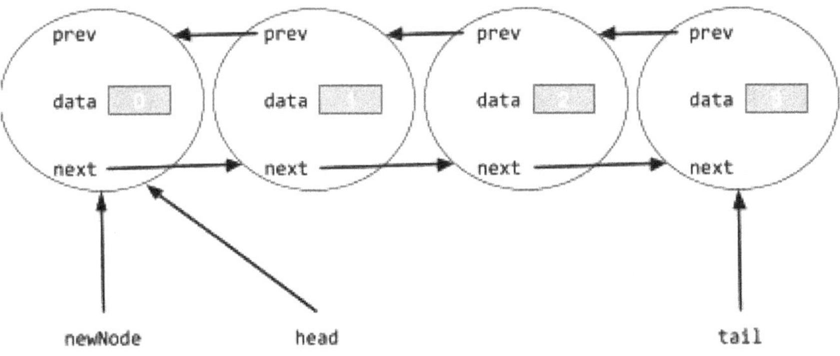

And like that, we have successfully inserted a new Node
at the beginning of the list.

The next case we will cover is when the Node needs to
be added at the end of the list. Similar to linking the

newNode before the head, we will be linking it after the
tail:

```
} else if(index == size) {
    newNode.prev = tail;
    tail.next = newNode;
    tail = newNode;
}
```

Take for example, the same list with 1, 2, 3, as above,
and let's say we wanted to add 4 to the end of the list:

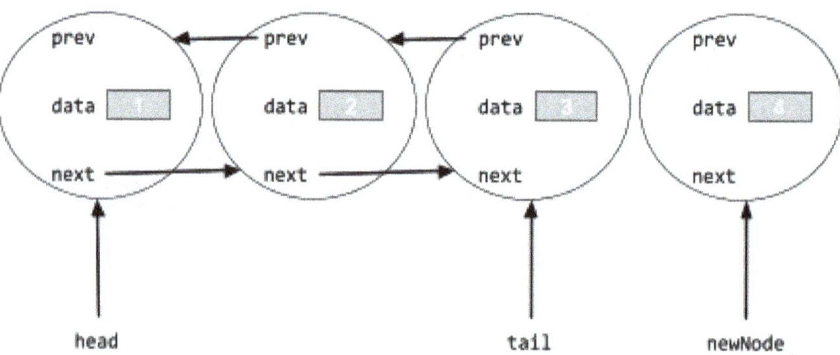

We first link the newNode and the tail:

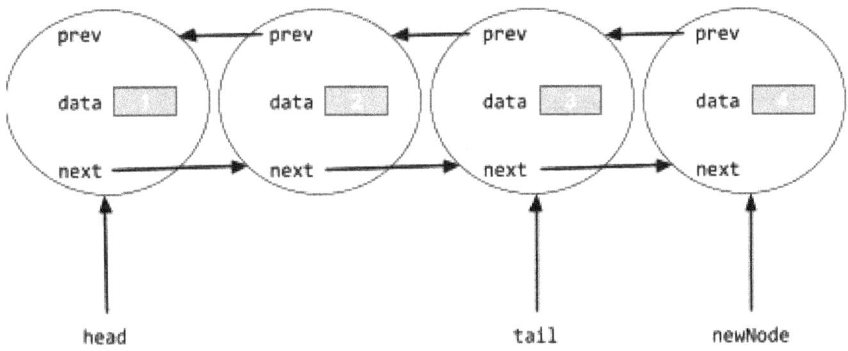

prev
data
next
prev
data
next
prev
data
next
prev
data
next
head
tail
newNode

Then, we move the `tail` pointer:

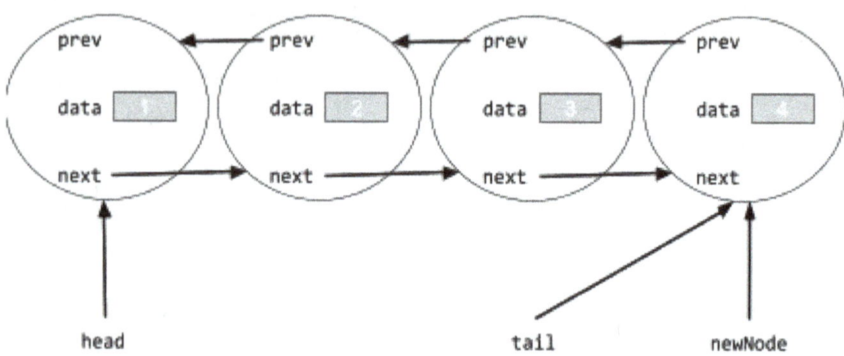

The third and final case to deal with is when we have to
insert somewhere in the middle of the list. This is where
we use the `getNode` method that we created earlier.

```
} else {
    Node curr = getNode(index);

}
```

newNode should go one **Node** immediately before curr, so
we will also need a reference to the previous **Node**:

```
Node prevNode = curr.prev;
```

Now we can link the **Nodes** together. First we link
newNode:

```
newNode.prev = prevNode;
newNode.next = curr;
```

Then we link the previous and next Nodes:

```
prevNode.next = newNode;
curr.prev = newNode;
```

Again, take the list 1,2,3 for example and let's say we wanted to add the element 8 at the index 1.

First we get pointers to the Node at index 1 as well as the Node before it, at index 0. For the sake of visual clarity, the head and tail pointers will be omitted:

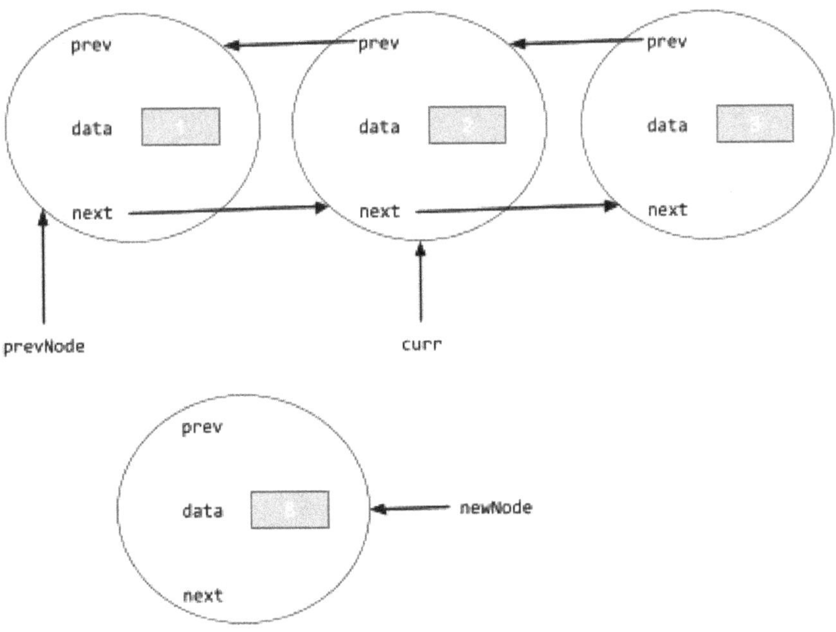

Now, we can start linking the nodes together. Let's first link newNode to its two potential neighbors:

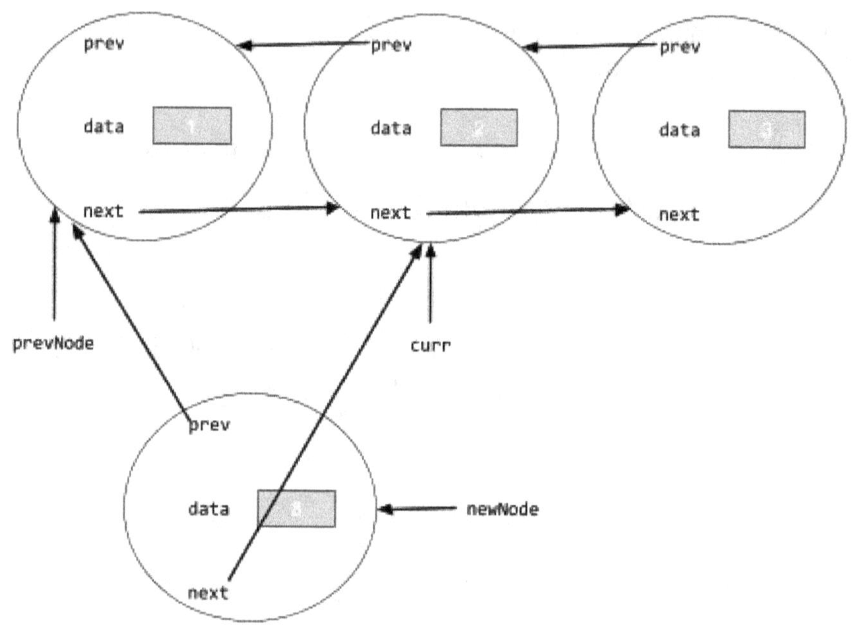

Then, link the neighbors back to newNode:

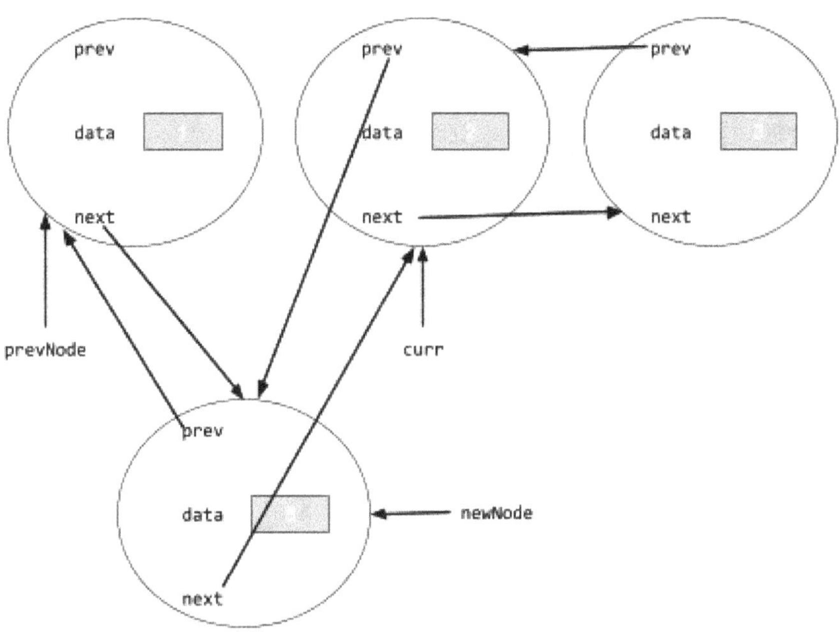

And we're done! The picture below shows the same LinkedList but just rearranged to make it look nicer:

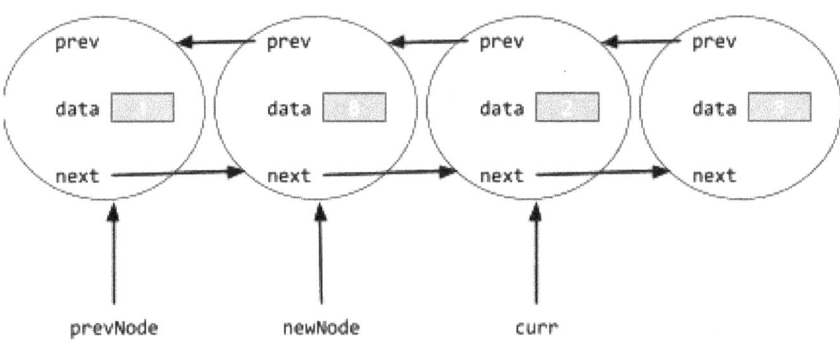

Now that every Node is connected, you can see that newNode has slotted in nicely between prevNode and curr and is now a part of the list.

Here is the whole add method:

```java
public void add(int index, int val) {
    checkIndex(index, true);

    Node newNode = new Node(val);
    size++;

    if(index == 0) {
        if(head == null)
            head = tail = newNode;
        else {
            head.prev = newNode;
            newNode.next = head;
            head = newNode;
        }
    } else if(index == size) {
        newNode.prev = tail;
        tail.next = newNode;
        tail = newNode;
    } else {
        Node curr = getNode(index);
        Node prevNode = curr.prev;
        newNode.prev = prevNode;
        newNode.next = curr;
        prevNode.next = newNode;
        curr.prev = newNode;
    }
}
```

Remove

Removing an element in a LinkedList is as simple as disconnecting that Node from the rest of the list. You can think of it as the reverse of adding a Node.

First, we get the Node that we want to remove.

Just like adding, there are 3 cases. The first is when you want to remove the first element, which is associated with the head Node:

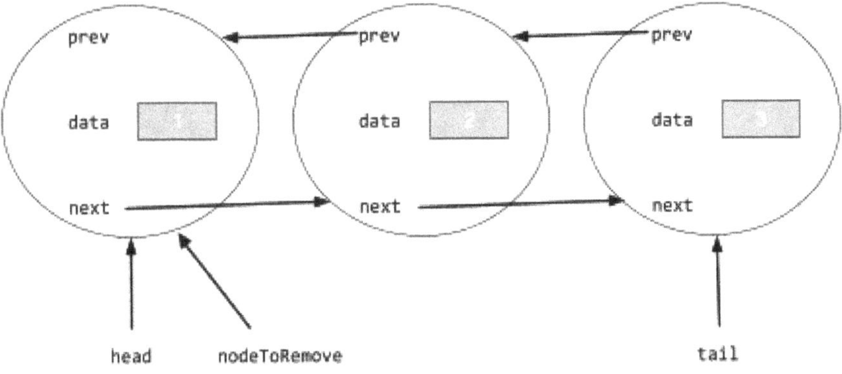

In that case, we move the head to the next Node:

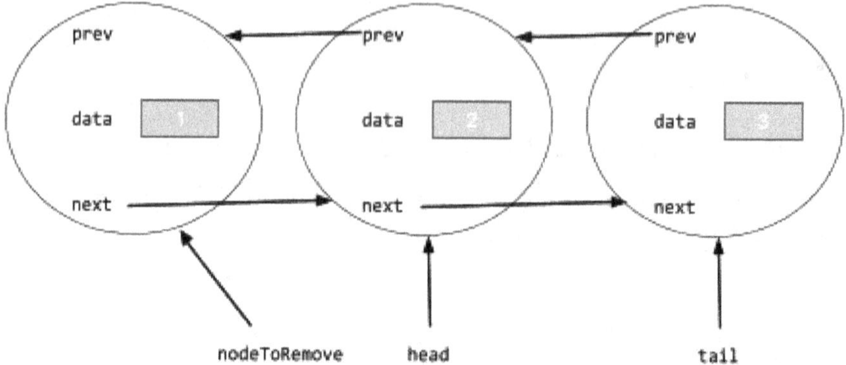

And then we set head.prev to null:

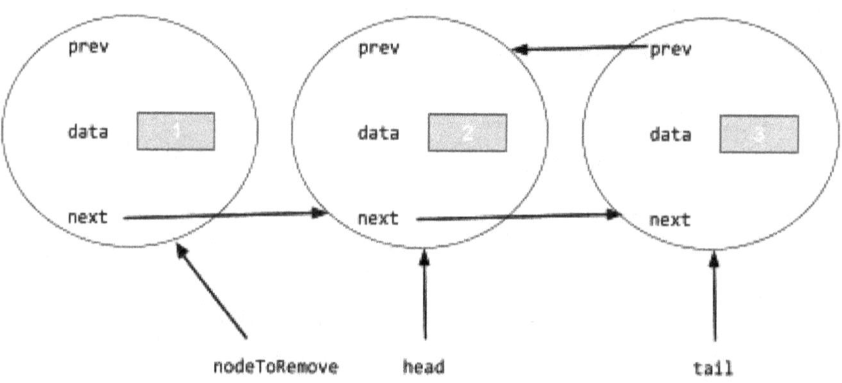

Finally, we set nodeToRemove.next to null:

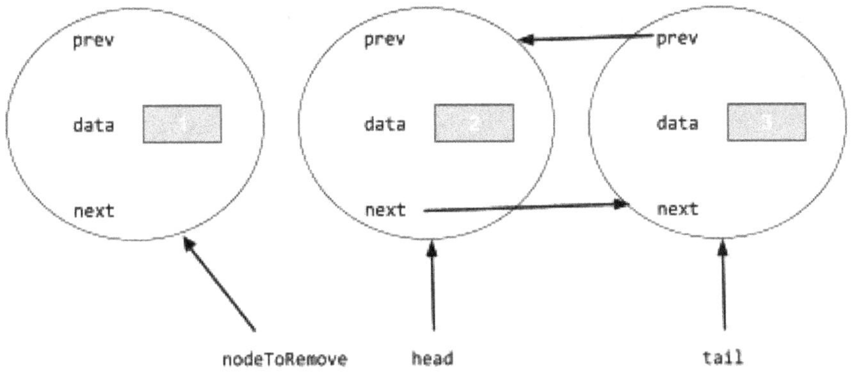

And with that, the nodeToRemove is not linked to the rest of the list anymore.

The second case is when we want to remove the **tail** of the list:

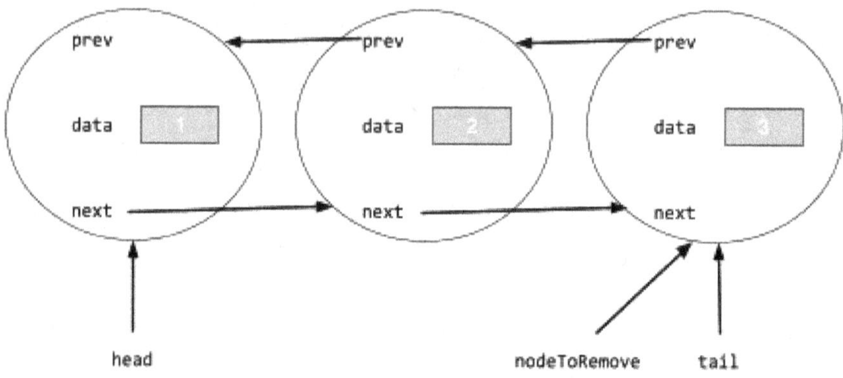

First we move the **tail** to the previous **Node**:

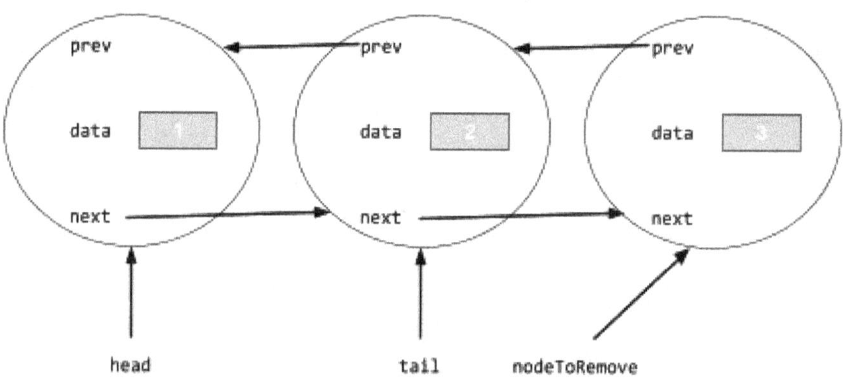

And we set `tail.next to null`:

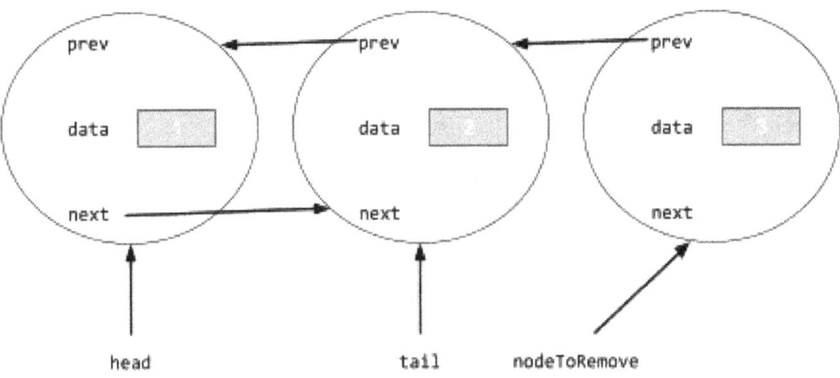

Finally, we set `nodeToRemove.prev` to `null`:

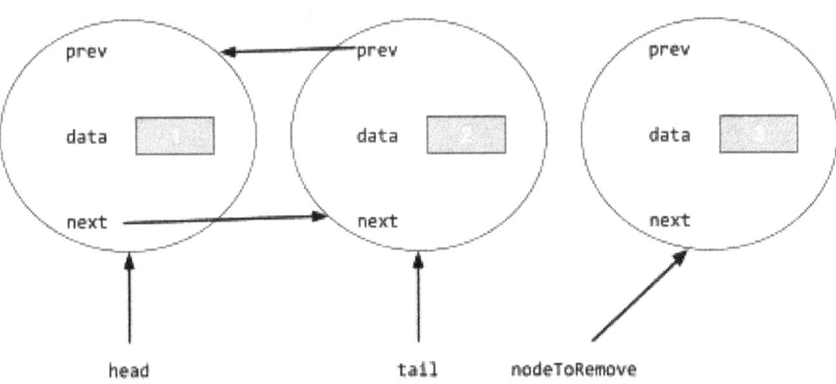

And now the Nodes can't connect to nodeToRemove and it is effectively disconnected from the list.

The third case is when `nodeToRemove` is in the middle of the list:

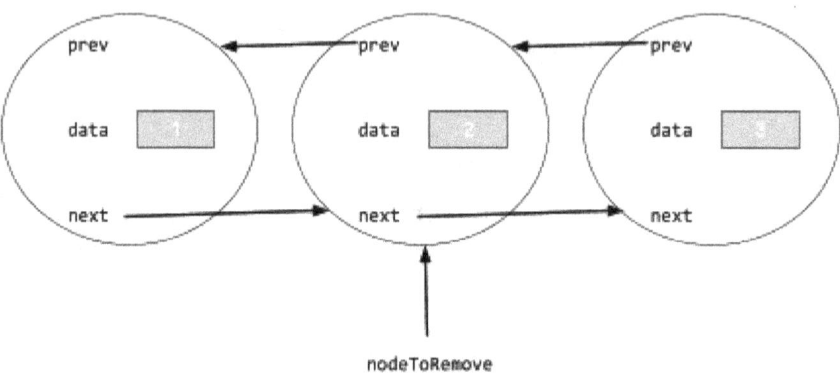

In that case, we get references to the `Nodes` before and after `nodeToRemove`:

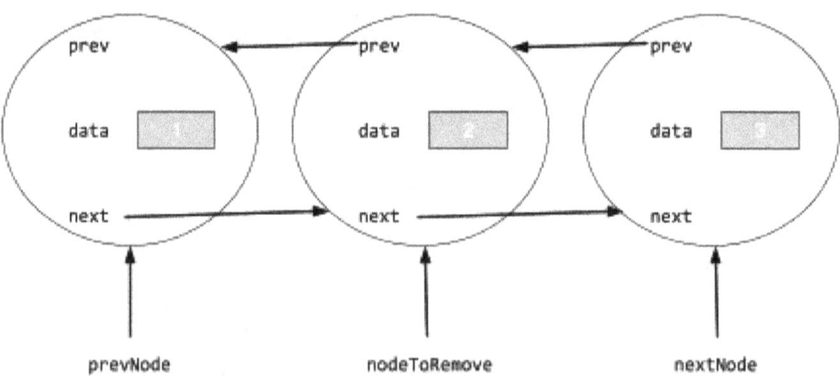

We then disconnect the middle node. This starts by changing `prevNode`'s next pointer:

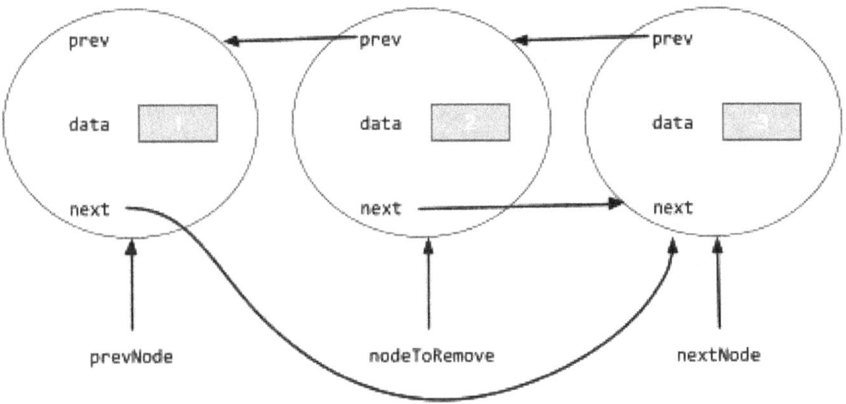

We also make `nextNode`'s prev pointer to skip over `nodeToRemove`:

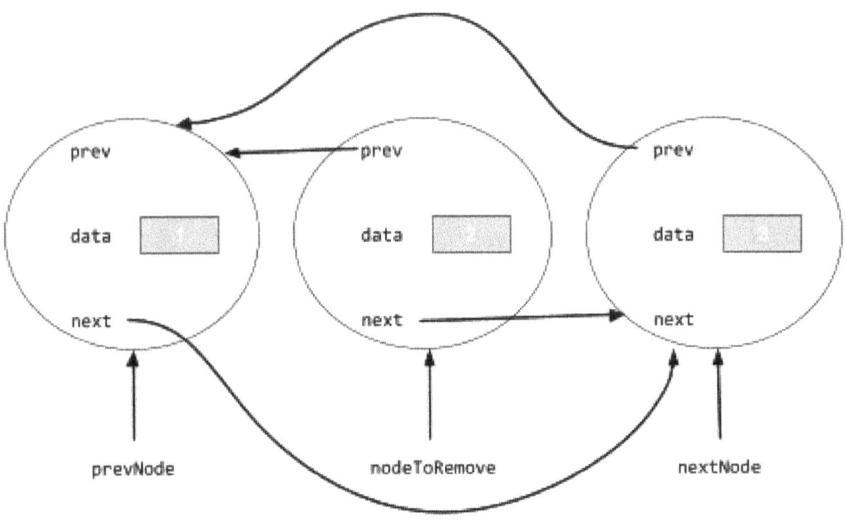

Finally, we set the prev and next pointers of
nodeToRemove to null:

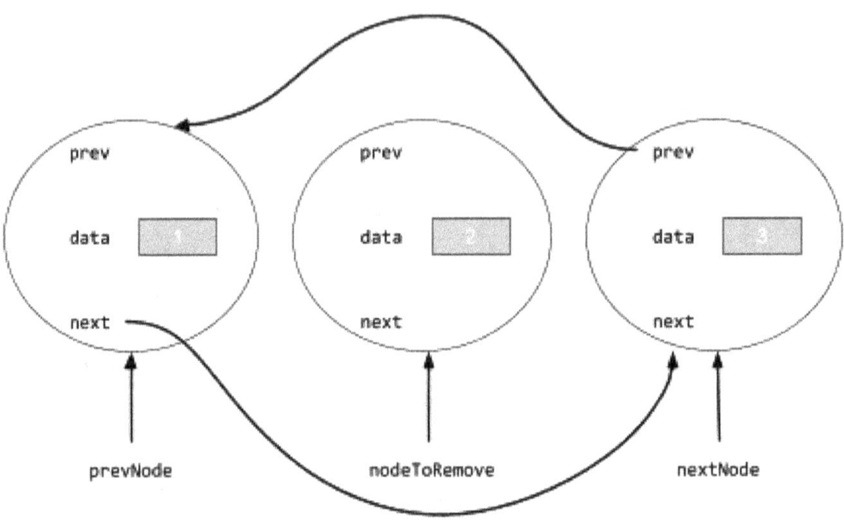

It might make things clearer if we take out nodeToRemove
from the picture:

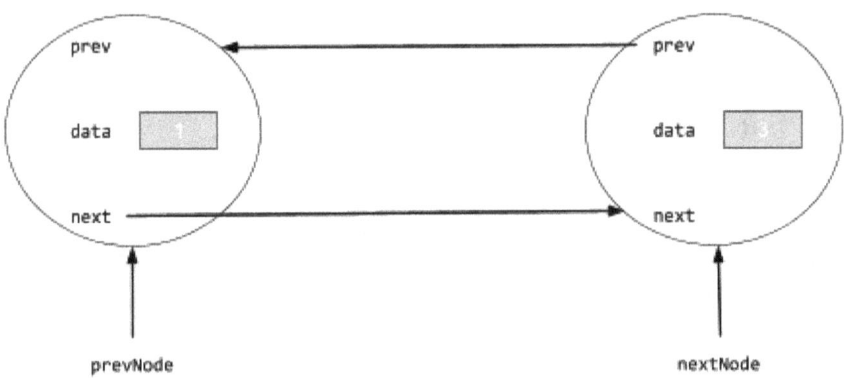

This is what we end up with. Notice how none of the Nodes connect to `nodeToRemove`, so it has been disconnected from the list.

And finally, the code:

```java
public void remove(int index) {
    checkIndex(index, false);

    Node nodeToRemove = getNode(index);

    if(nodeToRemove == head) {
        head = nodeToRemove.next;
        if(head != null) {
            head.prev = null;
            nodeToRemove.next = null;
        }
    } else if(nodeToRemove == tail) {
        tail = nodeToRemove.prev;
        tail.next = null;
        nodeToRemove.prev = null;
    } else {
        Node prevNode = nodeToRemove.prev;
        Node nextNode = nodeToRemove.next;
        prevNode.next = nextNode;
        nextNode.prev = prevNode;
        nodeToRemove.prev = null;
        nodeToRemove.next = null;
    }

    size--;
}
```

Get

Getting is a much simpler operation: we only need to check if the index is bounds and if it is, we retrieve the appropriate `Node` and return its value:

```java
public int get(int index) {
    checkIndex(index, false);
    Node node = getNode(index);
    return node.data;
}
```

Set

Likewise with setting a value, all that we need to do is change the appropriate `Node`'s value:

```java
public void set(int index, int data) {
    checkIndex(index, false);
    Node node = getNode(index);
    node.data = data;
}
```

Full Implementation

```java
public class MyLinkedList implements MyList {
    private Node head;
    private Node tail;
    private int size;

    private class Node {
```

```java
        int data;
        Node prev;
        Node next;

        public Node(int data) {
            this.data = data;
        }
    }

    private void checkIndex(int index, boolean
inclusive) {
        if(inclusive && index == size)
            return;

        if(index < 0 || index >= size)
            throw new IndexOutOfBoundsException(index
+ " is out of bounds.");
    }

    private Node getNode(int index) {
        Node curr;
        if(index < size / 2) {
            curr = head;
            for(int i = 0; i < index; i++)
                curr = curr.next;
        } else {
            curr = tail;
            for(int i = size - 1; i > index; i--)
                curr = curr.prev;
        }

        return curr;
    }
```

```java
public int size() {
    return size;
}

public void add(int data) {
    add(size, data);
}

public void add(int index, int val) {
    checkIndex(index, true);

    Node newNode = new Node(val);
    size++;

    if(index == 0) {
        if(head == null)
            head = tail = newNode;
        else {
            head.prev = newNode;
            newNode.next = head;
            head = newNode;
        }
    } else if(index == size) {
        newNode.prev = tail;
        tail.next = newNode;
        tail = newNode;
    } else {
        Node curr = getNode(index);
        Node prevNode = curr.prev;
        newNode.prev = prevNode;
        newNode.next = curr;
        prevNode.next = newNode;
        curr.prev = newNode;
    }
```

```java
    }

    public void remove(int index) {
        checkIndex(index, false);

        Node nodeToRemove = getNode(index);

        if(nodeToRemove == head) {
            head = nodeToRemove.next;
            if(head != null) {
                head.prev = null;
                nodeToRemove.next = null;
            }
        } else if(nodeToRemove == tail) {
            tail = nodeToRemove.prev;
            tail.next = null;
            nodeToRemove.prev = null;
        } else {
            Node prevNode = nodeToRemove.prev;
            Node nextNode = nodeToRemove.next;
            prevNode.next = nextNode;
            nextNode.prev = prevNode;
            nodeToRemove.prev = null;
            nodeToRemove.next = null;
        }

        size--;
    }

    public int get(int index) {
        checkIndex(index, false);
        Node node = getNode(index);
        return node.data;
    }
```

```java
    public void set(int index, int data) {
        checkIndex(index, false);
        Node node = getNode(index);
        node.data = data;
    }
}
```

Analysis of Time Complexities

size() – O(1)

add() – The `add()` methods in a LinkedList have different time complexities depending on the position of the insertion. When adding an element at the beginning or end of the list, the operation is O(1) as it involves updating references of only a few nodes. However, when adding an element at a specific index in the middle of the list, the operation requires traversing the list to find the appropriate position, making it O(n).

remove() – Similar to the `add()` method, the `remove()` operation in a LinkedList also depends on the position of the element being removed. If the removal is at the beginning or end of the list, the operation is O(1). However, if the element is in the middle, it requires traversing the list to find the element, resulting in an O(n) time complexity

get() and **set()** – Both of these methods have time complexities of O(n). This is because accessing or modifying an element at a specific index requires traversing the list from either the head or tail until reaching the desired index. In the best case, when accessing/modifying the first or last element, the complexity is O(1).

Use Cases

LinkedLists are useful when:
- You need a dynamic list that can grow or shrink
- You need to frequently add/remove/access elements at the beginning or end of the list since these operations are O(1)
- You need to implement data structures like Stacks and Queues. Under the hood, these abstract data types delegate their operations to a LinkedList. We'll cover Stacks and Queues in the next chapters.

Chapter Summary

In this chapter, we created a concrete implementation of MyList: MyLinkedList. Since it's a subclass of MyList, you can create instances of it like this:

```java
MyList myList = new MyLinkedList();
```

Similar to MyArrayList in the previous chapter, you can then add items to it, or you can remove from it. And since it's a list, you can always be sure that it maintains a certain order (i.e., insertion order). But most importantly, it can grow and shrink dynamically.

Unlike ArrayLists, LinkedLists store their data in nodes, with each node linked to the previous and next. And in general, they outperform ArrayLists when performing operations at or near the beginning of the list. This is because unlike an ArrayList, there is no shifting of elements during add/remove as would happen in an array. Instead, the nodes can be added in place. Thus, adding/removing elements at the beginning is O(1).

It is in the middle where the performance of add/remove becomes similar because in an ArrayList, elements need to shift forward/backward, while in a LinkedList, you need to iterate over the list in order to get to a specific node.

Chapter 5

MyQueue

Pretend you are standing in line to buy tickets to a movie. You may have heard this called a *queue*. A queue is a structured line of elements, and follows a principle known as First In, First Out (FIFO).

You can think of FIFO like this: the First person *into* the queue will be the first one processed, and the first person *out* of the queue. So, the first person to enter the line to buy a ticket will get their ticket first. Then, the second person will get their ticket, and etc. until the last person in line has gotten their ticket.

In Java, there is a class called Queue to represent this type of data structure; elements that are added first will be processed first, while elements that are added last will be processed last.

In this chapter, we create a class very similar to Java's. We call it MyQueue. Under the hood, it will actually be using a LinkedList due to the fact that it involves many operations at the beginning and the end of the structure. And a LinkedList provides O(1) operations when adding/removing at the beginning and end.

Let's start with a basic MyQueue class:

```java
public class MyQueue {
    MyLinkedList list = new MyLinkedList();

    public int size() {
        return size;
    }
}
```

Our Queue will have three more methods:

Offer

Our `offer()` method will represent an element being added to the end of the queue:

```java
public void offer(int data) {
    list.add(data);
}
```

We add the element to the end of the underlying LinkedList.

Peek

peek() will allow us to get the element at the front of the queue without removing it. Think of it like peeking at the front of the line.

```java
public int peek() {
```

```
    return list.get(0);
}
```

Poll

poll(), unlike peek(), will get the first element in the
queue and then remove it as well.

```
public int poll() {
    int data = peek();
    list.remove(0);
    return data;
}
```

Full Implementation

```
public class Queue {
    MyLinkedList list = new MyLinkedList();

    public int size() {
        return list.size();
    }

    public void offer(int data) {
        list.add(data);
    }

    public int peek() {
        return list.get(0);
    }

    public int poll() {
        int data = peek();
```

```java
        list.remove(0);
        return data;
    }
}
```

Analysis of Time Complexities

size() – O(1)

offer() – O(1): adding to the end of a LinkedList is always O(1).

peek() – O(1): looking at the first node of a LinkedList is O(1).

poll() – O(1): Getting and removing the first node is O(1) as well.

Use Cases

Queues are useful for:

- Resource Allocation: Queues can be used to manage resources such as CPU time or network bandwidth. Processes or data packets waiting for a resource are placed in a queue and processed when the resource becomes available.
- Print Queue: A print queue manages print jobs in the order they are submitted. This ensures that print jobs are processed in the order they are received.

Chapter Summary

In this chapter we implemented Queues. Queues are sequences of elements that follow the First In, First Out (FIFO) principle, similar to waiting in line to buy movie tickets. We used a LinkedList as the underlying data structure for a Queue because it provides O(1) operations for adding and removing elements at both the beginning and end.

Fundamental queue operations include `size()`, `offer()`, `peek()`, and `poll()`. Their time complexities are O(1) because they involve efficient operations on a LinkedList.

Chapter 6
MyStack

Stacks, unlike Queues, follow a First In, Last Out principle: the first element to enter the stack will be the last element to leave it.

Imagine a stack of plates at a restaurant. When you start stacking plates, the most recent plate is placed on top of the stack. As you continue to add plates, each new plate is added on top of the previous one. When you need to remove a plate from the stack, you'll always take the top plate first. The plate at the bottom of the stack will be the last one to be removed.

You can consider Stacks the counterparts to Queues. In a Queue, the first plate would be the first one to be taken out, whereas with a Stack, the first plate is the last one to be taken out.

Again, since there are so many operations at the top of a Stack, the data structure that should come to your mind should be a LinkedList, which will make our Stack methods O(1).

Here is the basic implementation of a Stack:

```java
public class MyStack {
    MyLinkedList list = new MyLinkedList();

    public int size() {
        return list.size();
    }
}
```

You may notice that this looks a lot like the Queue implementation already; Stacks and Queues are very similar data structures with only a few differences in their implementations of the following methods:

Push

Instead of having `offer()` as we do in a Queue, to add to the top of a Stack we will implement a method called `push()`:

```java
public void push(int val) {
    list.add(val);
}
```

We will treat the beginning of the list as the bottom of our stack and the end of the list as the top of our Stack, so pushing new elements to the top of the Stack will add them to the end of the list.

Peek

Just like a Queue, Stacks have a `peek()` method that allows you to see the top element. Since we said that the top of the stack would be the end, the implementation will slightly differ from that of a Queue:

```java
public int peek() {
    int n = size();
    return list.get(n - 1);
}
```

You can see that we need to look at the last element of the list, which means subtracting 1 from the list's `size` and looking at that element.

Pop

Our final method in this Stack is called pop. After you push elements to the top of the stack, you can pop them off (remove) in FILO order.

```java
public int pop() {
    int val = peek();

    int n = size();
    list.remove(n - 1);

    return val;
}
```

Again this implementation involves getting the last element before it is removed and returning it. This differs from our Queue code since in a Queue the element to be removed is at index 0 instead of the end of the list.

Full Implementation

```java
public class MyStack {
    MyLinkedList list = new MyLinkedList();

    public int size() {
        return list.size();
    }

    public void push(int val) {
        list.add(val);
    }

    public int peek() {
        int n = size();
        return list.get(n - 1);
    }

    public int pop() {
        int val = peek();

        int n = size();
        list.remove(n - 1);

        return val;
    }
}
```

Note that Queues and Stacks both have very simple implementations since they both build on the existing functionalities provided by LinkedLists.

Analysis of Time Complexities

`size()` – O(1)
`push()` – O(1)
`peek()` – O(1)
`pop()` – O(1)

Use Cases

- Method Call Management: Stacks are used in programming to manage method calls. When a method is called, its information is pushed onto the call stack, and when it returns, it's popped off. This allows the program to remember where to return after the method finishes.
- Undo/Redo Functionality: Stacks can be used to implement undo and redo functionality in applications. Every time an action is taken, the state is pushed onto the take, and when you undo that action, you pop off that action. If you choose to redo that action, then you would push the state back onto the stack.
- Browser Back Button: The back button in web browsers uses a stack to keep track of previously visited pages. Clicking "back" pops the current

page from the stack, returning you to the previous one, while clicking
"forward" pushes that page back onto the stack.

Chapter Summary

In this chapter, we implemented Stacks. Stacks are different from Queues because instead of FIFO, they use LIFO. Thus, the most recent item added to the stack is placed on top, and the top item is the first to be removed.

Again, our implementation used a LinkedList, with the top of the stack corresponding to the end of the list. Key stack operations include `size()`, `push()`, `peek()`, and `pop()`. These operations have O(1) time complexity due to the efficient LinkedList implementation.

Chapter 7

Binary Search Trees

Our final data structure is the Binary Search Tree, often abbreviated as BST. Binary Search Trees are very different from the other data structures that you have seen so far in that instead of being a linear representation of elements, its elements are stored in a structure that looks like a **tree**, hence the name.

This is probably not intuitive to you, so let's go over how a tree is constructed.

A tree in real life has roots in the ground, and then it grows up and branches out, and those branches might have more branches, until eventually the branches end up in leaves.

A Binary Search Tree is composed of nodes. It is called a BINARY Search Tree because each node in the tree has pointers to two other nodes: a left and a right. We call these pointers children, so each node can have a left child and a right child.

In addition, each node in the tree contains a value, just like a LinkedList node.

The tree has a node called root, which is the top node of
the tree.

Here is what a filled-out Binary Search Tree might look
like:

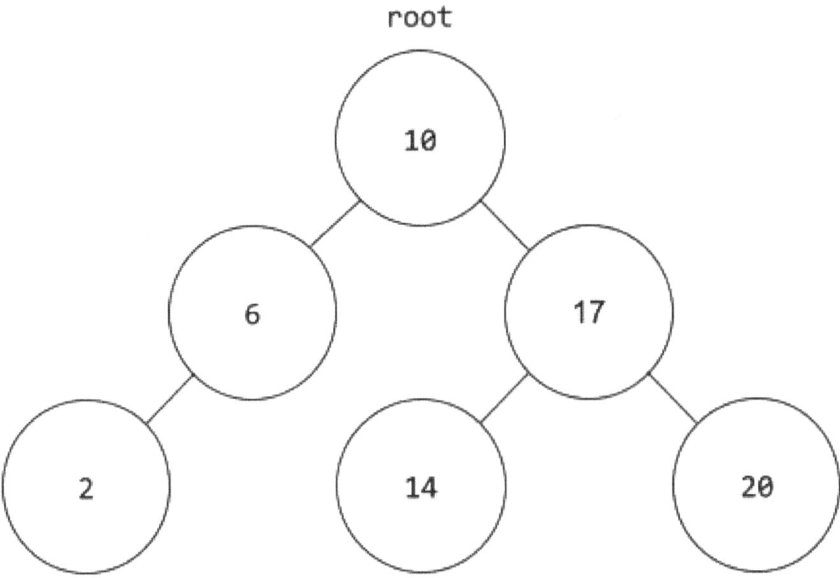

Notice how the root is the top Node in the tree, similar to
the head of a LinkedList. A node with no children is
called a **leaf**—so 2, 14, and 20 are leaves.

The most important characteristics of a Binary Search
Tree are:

1. For any node that you choose, all nodes to the left
   will be smaller in value.
2. For any node that you choose, all nodes to the
   right will be greater in value.
3. No duplicate elements are allowed.

You can see that this is true in the tree above. The root
node is 10, and all nodes in the left subtree (the tree
rooted at the node 6) have values that are less than 10.

Likewise, every node in the right subtree–17, 14, and
20–is greater than 10.

You can see that this holds true even when the node you
choose is not the root. For example, take the node 17:
14 < 17, while 20 > 17.

This feature is an essential one and you will see how it
becomes useful later.

Now let's take a look at a basic implementation of a
Binary Search Tree.

```java
public class BinarySearchTree {
    private TreeNode root;
    private int size;

    private static class TreeNode {
        int data;
        TreeNode left;
```

```java
        TreeNode right;

        public TreeNode(int data) {
            this.data = data;
        }
    }

    public int size() {
        return size;
    }
}
```

Here you can see that we have implemented a basic
TreeNode helper class that will represent a node in the
tree.

With that, we can finally start creating an **add** method.

Add

First let's take care of the base case, which is when the
tree is empty and you add the first node:

```java
public void add(int data) {
    if(root == null) {
        size++;
        root = new TreeNode(data);
        return;
    }
}
```

Now we can handle the more common case: when you want to add to a tree that already has nodes in it.

Remember, we want to maintain the condition that every node's left children are smaller than it, and its right children are greater than it. This also means that duplicate elements aren't allowed. What this means is we have to figure out where exactly in the tree to insert a node before adding it there:

```java
TreeNode prev = null;
TreeNode curr = root;

while(curr != null) {
    prev = curr;

    if(data < curr.data)
        curr = curr.left;
    else if(data > curr.data)
        curr = curr.right;
    else
        return;
}

size++;
if(data < prev.data)
    prev.left = new TreeNode(data);
else
    prev.right = new TreeNode(data);
```

Let's break this down with an example. Suppose we wanted to add a new node with the value of 15. First, take some time and decide where that node should go in the tree.

Now let's do it following the code. First, we start with two pointers: prev, and curr. curr starts at the root, while prev will be following curr.

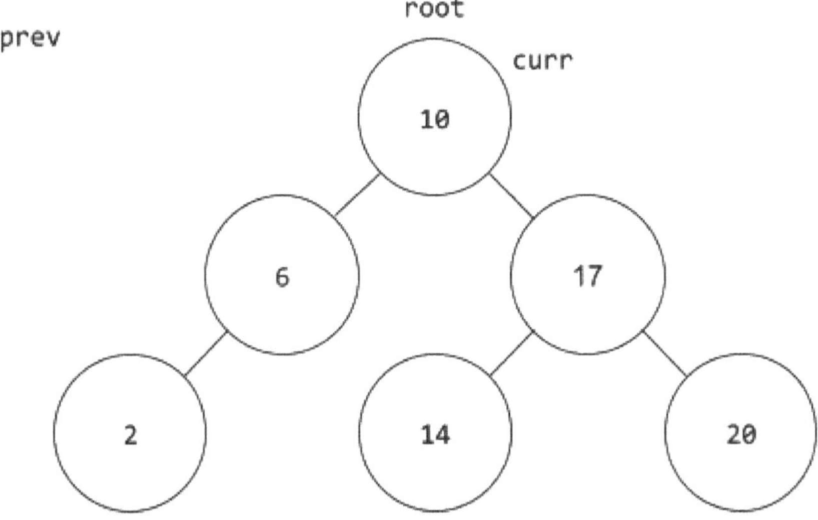

Note that prev is not pointing to anything right now.

With the first iteration of the loop, we look to see where the new TreeNode should be inserted.

First we assign **prev** to the `TreeNode` that **curr** is on.
Then, we compare **data** to `curr.data`. Since 15 is greater
than 10, we proceed to the right.

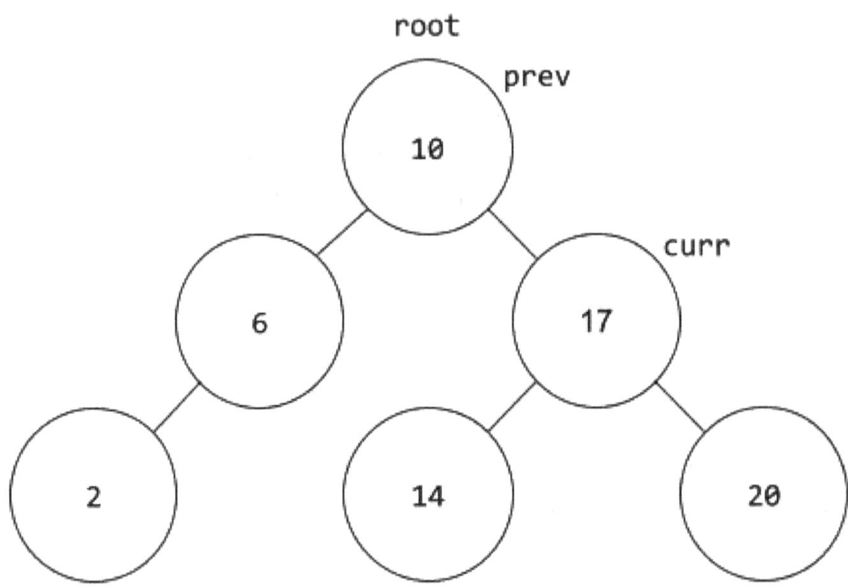

Now you might begin to see how **prev** will be tracking
curr and stay one step behind it.

With the next iteration of the loop, we see that 15 is less
than 17, so we move **curr** and **prev** accordingly:

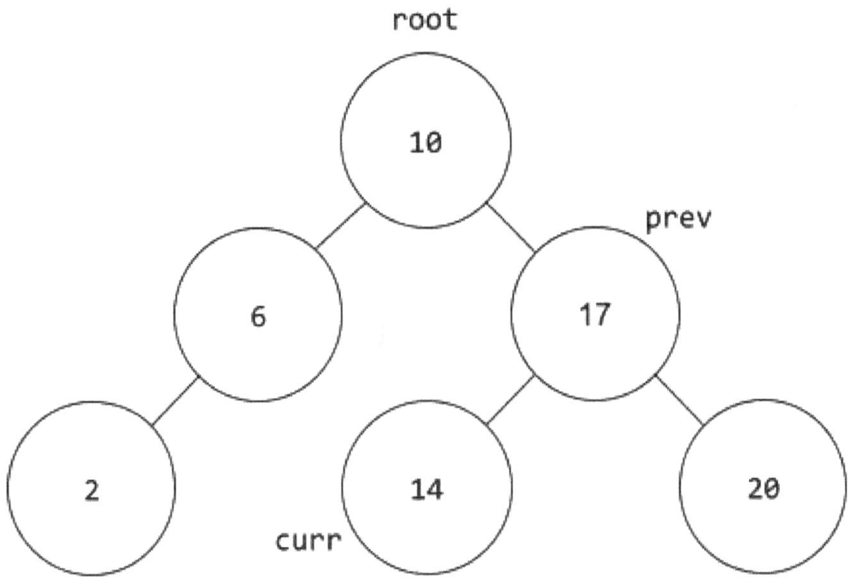

For the final iteration of our loop, we check if 15 is greater than or less than 14. Since it is greater, we will move curr to the right and move prev accordingly.

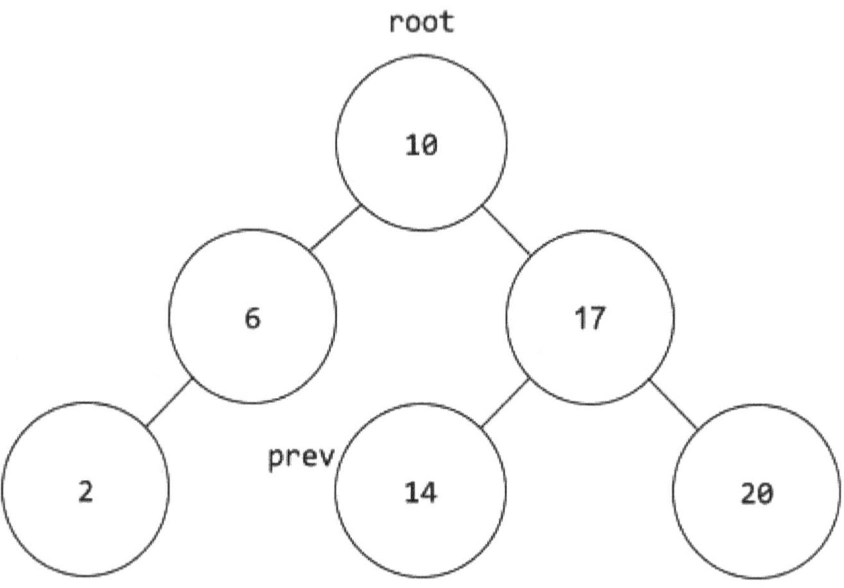

Hopefully now it becomes clear why we had to go through that loop, as now we know where to insert the new Node. We compare 15 to `prev.data`, find out that it is greater, and then insert a new `TreeNode` to the right accordingly:

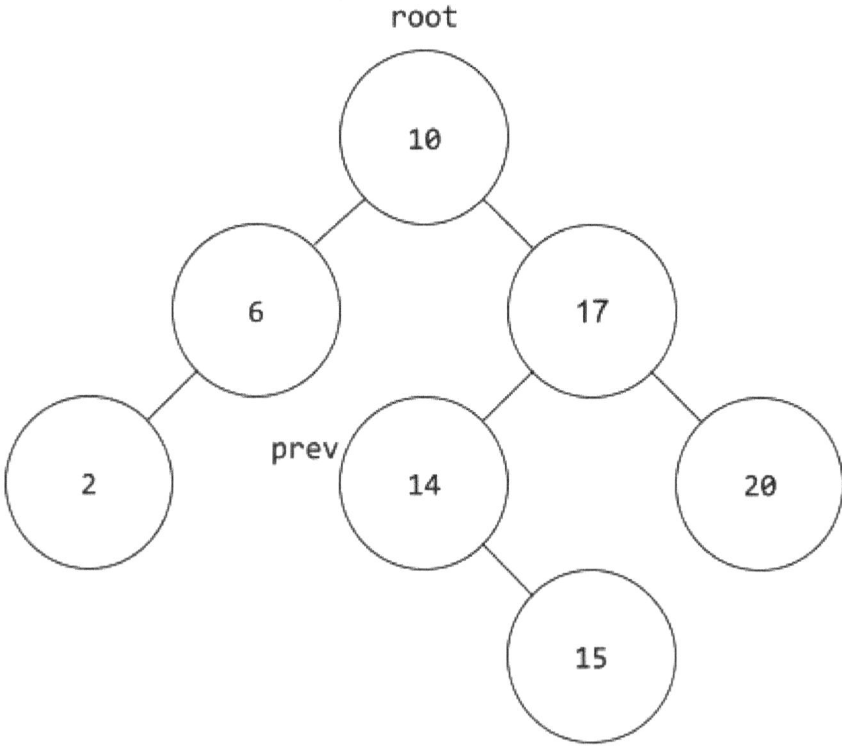

And just like that we have added 15 to our tree! As you add more data to the tree, notice that 1) there are no duplicates in the tree, and 2) new nodes are always added as leaves.

Remove

Removing a node from the tree is a bit more complicated than adding but follows the same basic procedure.

For this method, we will invoke a helper method called
`deleteNode`. You will see why later:

```java
public void remove(int data) {
    root = deleteNode(root, data, false);
}

private TreeNode deleteNode(TreeNode node, int data,
boolean shouldDecreaseSize) {
}
```

As the name implies, `deleteNode` will actually delete a
node containing the data within the tree. The method
takes in a `TreeNode` parameter indicating where to start
looking for the data. The `shouldDecreaseSize` flag is used
to determine whether or not to decrement the size of
the BST.

As you can imagine, removing a node can cause the tree
or its subtrees to be rearranged. After seeing how this
rearrangement happens, you'll come to understand why
the return type of `deleteNode` is also a `TreeNode`.

Let's start with the base case, where the `TreeNode`
passed in is `null`:

```java
if(node == null)
    return node;
```

If the node is not `null`, then we examine the data to be deleted. If its value is smaller than the current node's value, we'll need to visit the left subtree and remove the appropriate node. The same goes for if the value is greater.

```
if(data < node.data)
    node.left = deleteNode(node.left, data,
shouldDecreaseSize);
else if(data > node.data)
    node.right = deleteNode(node.right, data,
shouldDecreaseSize);
```

Note that visiting the left or right subtree is actually a recursive call – if the data is not found in the current node, we go deeper one level. When we come back out from the level below, we assign the left/right pointer the node being returned. Why? Because, as you'll see in the code later, the removal of a node can cause rearrangement.

The final scenario is when the current node does contain the value that we want to delete. When this happens, there are 3 cases to consider:

Case 1 is when the node to remove does not have any children (i.e., it's a leaf). If true, we can just `return null` because we want to disconnect this leaf node from its parent.

Case 2 is when the node to remove has only one child. In this case, we will return the non-null child, so it will replace the current node (i.e., it becomes the root of the subtree).

We also need to decrement the size when deleting a node from the tree, so we'll do that here with the help of the `shouldDecreaseSize` boolean. As mentioned previously, this flag tells us whether we should decrease the size or not. You will see why this is important later.

We can account for the first two cases with some simple code:

```java
else {
    if(shouldDecreaseSize)
        size--;

    if(node.left == null)
        return node.right;
    else if(node.right == null)
        return node.left;

    // Implement Case 3 here
}
```

If one child is `null`, then we return the other. If both children are `null`, then it doesn't matter which one we return as both are `null` either way.

Finally we can tackle the 3rd case, which is when the node to remove has two children. This is tough because it's not immediately clear what to replace the node with.

Remember, the value that replaces the current node needs to satisfy the condition of the BST - any value in the left subtree must be smaller than the current value, and any value in the right subtree must be greater than the current value. So we are tasked with finding a node that satisfies both these conditions.

One way is to find the successor node. Namely, we need to find the node with the smallest value in the right subtree. How do we do this? Consider the following tree:

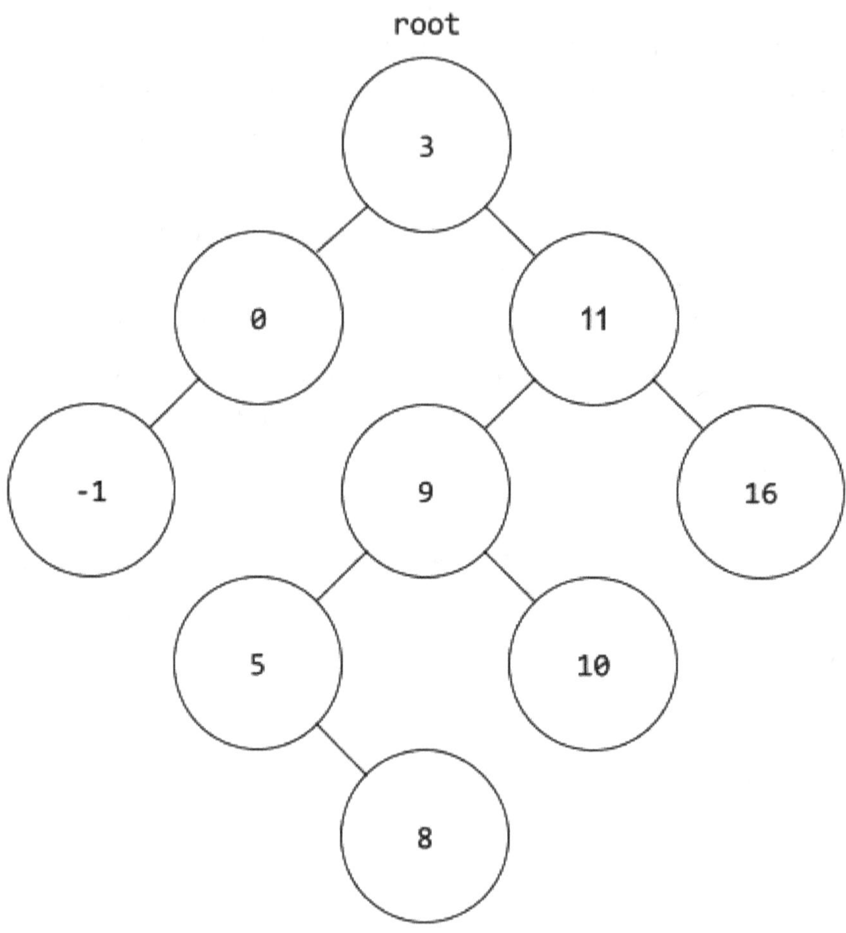

Let's say we wanted to delete the root node, 3, which has two children. Which node do we select that is the successor to 3? Well, the algorithm goes like this:

- First, go to the right child
- Then, go as far left as you can

Starting at node 3, we go right to node 11, and then go left to 9, and then to 5. Thus, 5 is the successor. You can also see that 5 is greater than all the nodes in the left subtree of 3, but it is less than all the nodes in the right subtree of 3.

So let's go back to the code. Before adding more to our `deleteNode` method, let's create a `findSuccessor` method that will return the successor of a node with two children:

```java
private int findSuccessor(TreeNode node) {
    TreeNode curr = node.right;
    while(curr.left != null)
        curr = curr.left;

    return curr.data;
}
```

Now that we can find the successor, we need to replace the current node's value with the successor's value in the `deleteNode` method:

```java
int successor = findSuccessor(node);
node.data = successor;
```

You might notice something's a bit off, though. Using the same example as earlier, the tree becomes this:

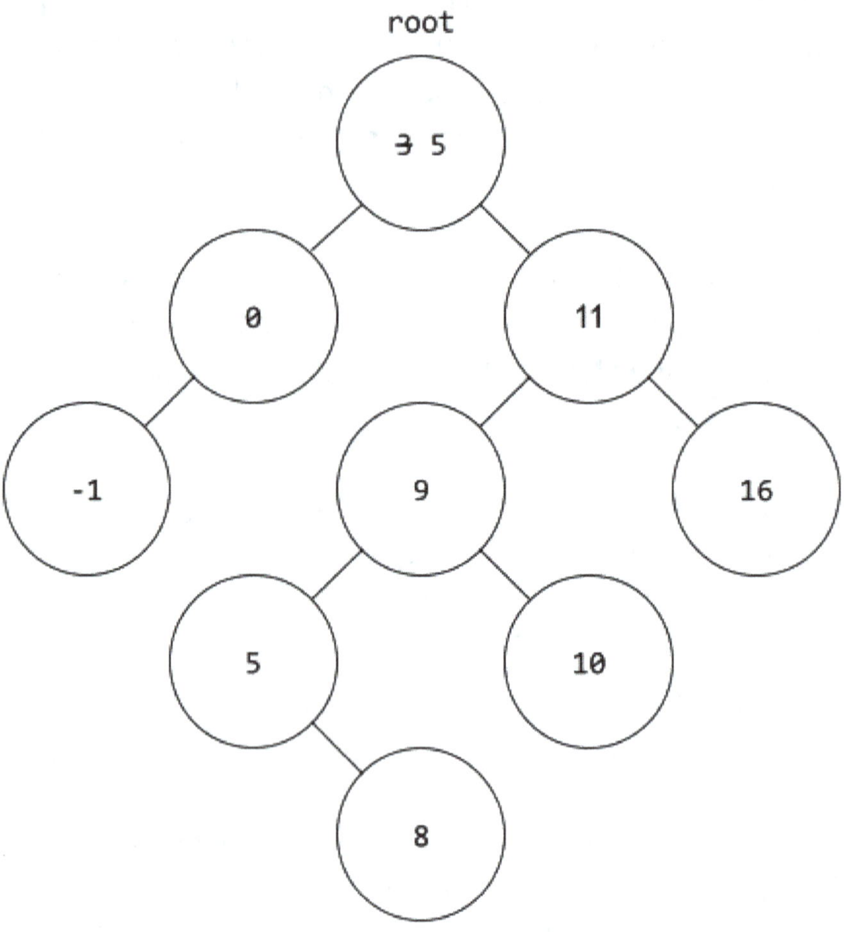

The 3 has been deleted from the tree, but now we have
a duplicate 5. So what we can do is call `deleteNode`
again, and remove the original successor node from the
tree:

```
node.right = deleteNode(node.right, successor,
false);
```

Also note that since we already have decremented the size, there's no need to do it again when we reach the successor node, so we'll set `shouldDecreaseSize` to `false`.

And after that whole process, the data value 3 has been removed from the tree, and the 8 becomes the left child of 9.

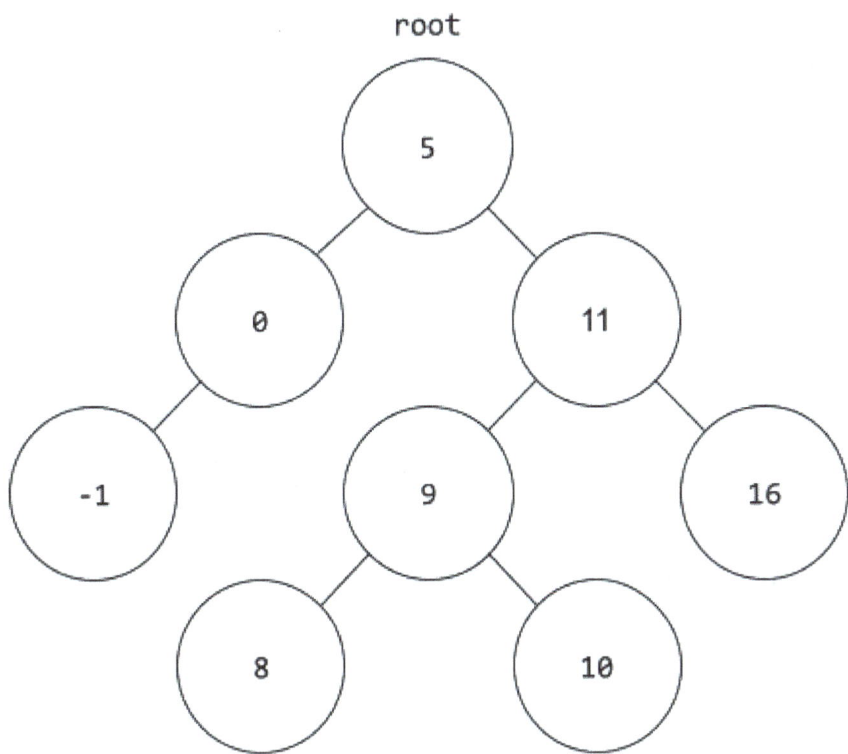

Here is the full `deleteNode` method:

```java
private TreeNode deleteNode(TreeNode node, int data,
boolean shouldDecreaseSize) {
    if(node == null)
        return node;

    if(data < node.data)
        node.left = deleteNode(node.left, data,
shouldDecreaseSize);
    else if(data > node.data)
        node.right = deleteNode(node.right, data,
shouldDecreaseSize);
    else {
        if(shouldDecreaseSize)
            size--;

        if(node.left == null)
            return node.right;
        if(node.right == null)
            return node.left;

        int successor = findSuccessor(node);
        node.data = successor;
        node.right = deleteNode(node.right,
successor, false);
    }

    return node;
}
```

Search

The reason why we call it a Binary SEARCH Tree is that it's very easy to test an element's presence in the tree. To search for an element, we will use the same algorithm as defined in the add method.

```java
public boolean search(int data) {
    TreeNode curr = root;
    while(curr != null && data != curr.data) {
        if(data < curr.data)
            curr = curr.left;
        else
            curr = curr.right;
    }

    if(curr == null)
        return false;

    return true;
}
```

Note that since we don't need access to the `curr`'s parent, we don't need a `prev` pointer. We simply search the tree for `data` and find the appropriate position. If the node with that `data` value exists, we `return true`, but if it's `null` (doesn't exist), we `return false`.

Traversal

A Binary Search Tree isn't as easy to traverse as a list or an array; since there are no indices to access elements at, you can't just use a loop to go through a tree. Instead, we will be implementing two methods that will allow us to traverse a tree in different ways.

First we will look at breadth-first traversal. Breadth-first traversal is basically going through a tree level-by-level. It involves going to the first level (the root), and then the second level left to right (`root.left`, `root.right`), and then the third level left to right, and so on.

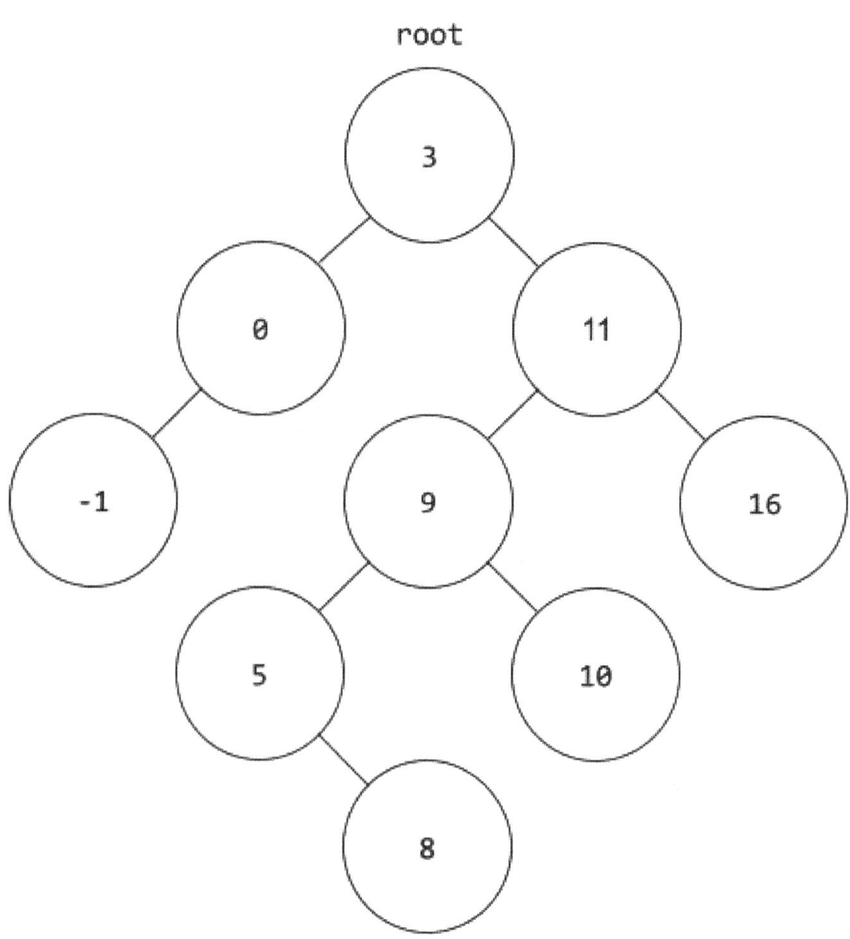

root
3
0
11
-1
9
16
5
10
8

The breadth-first traversal of the above tree would
result in:

Level 0: 3
Level 1: 0, 11
Level 2: -1, 9, 16
Level 3: 5, 10
Level 4: 8

Our implementation will use a `Queue` to store `TreeNodes`.
We will be using a `java.util.LinkedList` as our `Queue`
since it provides more functionality that our
implementation lacks:

```java
import java.util.Queue;
import java.util.LinkedList;
```

Now we can start our `breadthFirstTraverse()` method:

```java
public void breadthFirstTraverse() {
    Queue<TreeNode> queue = new LinkedList<>();
    queue.offer(root);
}
```

Offering the `root` to the `queue` first represents going
through the first level.

For each node that we traverse, we have to add its
children to the end of the queue so that all nodes on the

current level are processed before we move on to the
next level:

```java
while(!queue.isEmpty()) {
    TreeNode node = queue.poll();

    if(node == null)
        continue;

    System.out.print(node.data + " ");
    queue.offer(node.left);
    queue.offer(node.right);
}
```

Consider the tree shown earlier. First, we offer the root
node 3. We enter the loop, popping out the node and
printing it. Then we add its left and right children: 0 and
11. Now we go back through the loop again, and add 0's
children to the end, and then 11's children to the end as
well. Then we go through the 3rd layer, and so on, until
we reach the end of the queue. You can see how each
level is traversed fully before moving on to TreeNodes on
the next level.

Another way to traverse a Binary Search Tree that we
will cover is called Depth-First Traversal. This method
differs from Breadth-First Traversal in that it goes all the
way as deep as it can into the tree before slowly
backtracking and processing elements as it goes, until it
goes back to the top.

There are three main ways to do an Depth-First Traversal: **preorder**, **inorder**, and **postorder**.

Inorder traverses the left subtree, then the root, then the right subtree, in that order.

Preorder traverses the root, then the left subtree, then the right subtree.

Postorder traverses the left subtree, then the right subtree, and then finally the root.

Consider this tree:

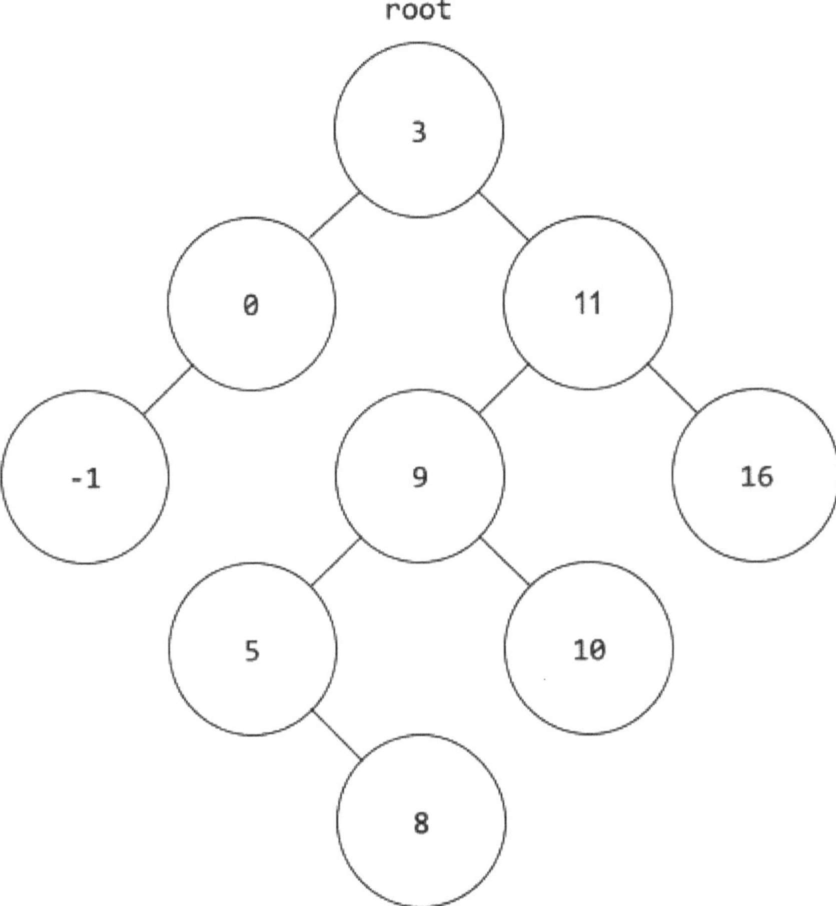

A preorder traversal traverses the node that you are currently on, then the left recursively, and then the right recursively:
{3, 0, -1, 11, 9, 5, 8, 10, 16}

Inorder traverses the entire left subtree before the current node, and then the entire right subtree:

```
{-1, 0, 3, 5, 8, 9, 10, 11, 16}
```

Postorder traverses the entire left and right subtrees before the current node:
```
{-1, 0, 8, 5, 10, 9, 16, 11, 3}
```

For the purposes of this book we will only be implementing inorder traversal. The benefit to using inorder is that it spits out elements in sorted order.

You can implement this using either an iterative or a recursive approach. Let's start with recursive:

```java
public void inOrderTraverse() {
    inOrderRecursive(root);
}

private void inOrderRecursive(TreeNode node) {
    if(node == null)
        return;
}
```

To output the nodes in sorted order, we first need to explore the nodes in the left subtree since they are less than the current TreeNode:

```java
inOrderRecursive(node.left);
```

Now that the left subtree is done, we can print the value
of the current node:

```java
System.out.print(node.data + " ");
```

Then we will explore the right subtree since it is greater
than the current Node:

```java
inOrderRecursive(node.right);
```

The full method looks like this:

```java
public void inOrderTraverse() {
    inOrderRecursive(root);
}

private void inOrderTraverseRecursive(TreeNode node)
{
    if(node == null)
        return;

    inOrderRecursive(node.left);
    System.out.print(node.data + " ");
    inOrderRecursive(node.right);
}
```

We can implement the same thing using the following
iterative version. First, we go as far left as we can and
add those elements to a Stack. What we're really doing
is we're mimicking the runtime stack of the recursive
method calls in the previous solution.

We pop each element in the stack and print its value. If that element (i.e., node) has a right child, we visit its leftmost child, adding nodes along the way. Thus, we're essentially finding the successor to the current value.

Here's the code:

```java
import java.util.Stack;

private void inOrderIterative() {
    Stack<TreeNode> stack = new Stack<>();
    TreeNode curr = root;

    // Go all the way left
    while(curr != null) {
        stack.push(curr);
        curr = curr.left;
    }

    while(stack.size() > 0) {
        curr = stack.pop();
        System.out.print(curr.data + " ");

        if(curr.right != null) {
            curr = curr.right;

            // Go all the way left
            while(curr != null) {
                stack.push(curr);
                curr = curr.left;
            }
```

```java
        }
    }
}
```

Full Implementation

```java
import java.util.Queue;
import java.util.Stack;
import java.util.LinkedList;

public class BinarySearchTree {
    private int size;
    private TreeNode root;

    private static class TreeNode {
        int data;
        TreeNode left;
        TreeNode right;

        public TreeNode(int data) {
            this.data = data;
        }
    }

    public int size() {
        return size;
    }

    public void add(int data) {
        TreeNode newNode = new TreeNode(data);

        if(root == null) {
            size++;
```

```java
            root = newNode;
            return;
        }

        TreeNode prev = null;
        TreeNode curr = root;

        while(curr != null) {
            prev = curr;

            if(data < curr.data)
                curr = curr.left;
            else if(data > curr.data)
                curr = curr.right;
            else // Ignore duplicates
                return;
        }

        size++;

        if(data < prev.data)
            prev.left = newNode;
        else
            prev.right = newNode;
    }

    public boolean search(int data) {
        TreeNode curr = root;

        while(curr != null) {
            if(data < curr.data)
                curr = curr.left;
            else if(data > curr.data)
                curr = curr.right;
```

```java
            else
                return true;
        }

        return false;
    }


    public void remove(int data) {
        root = deleteNode(root, data, true);
    }


    private TreeNode deleteNode(TreeNode node, int
data, boolean shouldDecreaseSize) {
        if(node == null)
            return node;

        if(data < node.data)
            node.left = deleteNode(node.left, data,
shouldDecreaseSize);
        else if(data > node.data)
            node.right = deleteNode(node.right, data,
shouldDecreaseSize);
        else {
            if(shouldDecreaseSize)
                size--;

            if(node.left == null)
                return node.right;
            if(node.right == null)
                return node.left;

            int successor = findSuccessor(node);
            node.data = successor;
            node.right = deleteNode(node.right,
```

```java
successor, false);
        }

        return node;
    }


    private int findSuccessor(TreeNode node) {
        TreeNode curr = node.right;
        while(curr.left != null)
            curr = curr.left;

        return curr.data;
    }


    public void breadthFirstTraverse() {
        Queue<TreeNode> queue = new LinkedList<>();
        queue.offer(root);

        while(!queue.isEmpty()) {
            TreeNode node = queue.poll();

            if(node == null)
                continue;

            System.out.print(node.data + " ");
            queue.offer(node.left);
            queue.offer(node.right);
        }
    }


    public void inOrderTraverse() {
        inOrderRecursive(root);
        //inOrderIterative();
    }
```

```java
private void inOrderRecursive(TreeNode node) {
    if(node == null)
        return;

    inOrderRecursive(node.left);
    System.out.print(node.data + " ");
    inOrderRecursive(node.right);
}

private void inOrderIterative() {
    Stack<TreeNode> stack = new Stack<>();
    TreeNode curr = root;

    // Go all the way left
    while(curr != null) {
        stack.push(curr);
        curr = curr.left;
    }

    while(stack.size() > 0) {
        curr = stack.pop();
        System.out.print(curr.data + " ");

        if(curr.right != null) {
            curr = curr.right;

            // Go all the way left
            while(curr != null) {
                stack.push(curr);
                curr = curr.left;
            }
        }
    }
}
```

    }
}

Analysis of Time Complexities

add() - Usually is O(log n) since usually we have to traverse through `log` n levels to get to the leaf node where we can add a child. Basically, this is the height of the tree.
remove() – Also is usually O(log n) for the same reason.
search() – O(log n) for the same reason.
Breadth-First and Depth-First Traversal – O(n) since it goes through every node.

Note that in an unbalanced BST, like the one shown below, the time complexity will become O(n) as this essentially becomes a LinkedList, where you have to go through all the nodes to get to the leaf node.

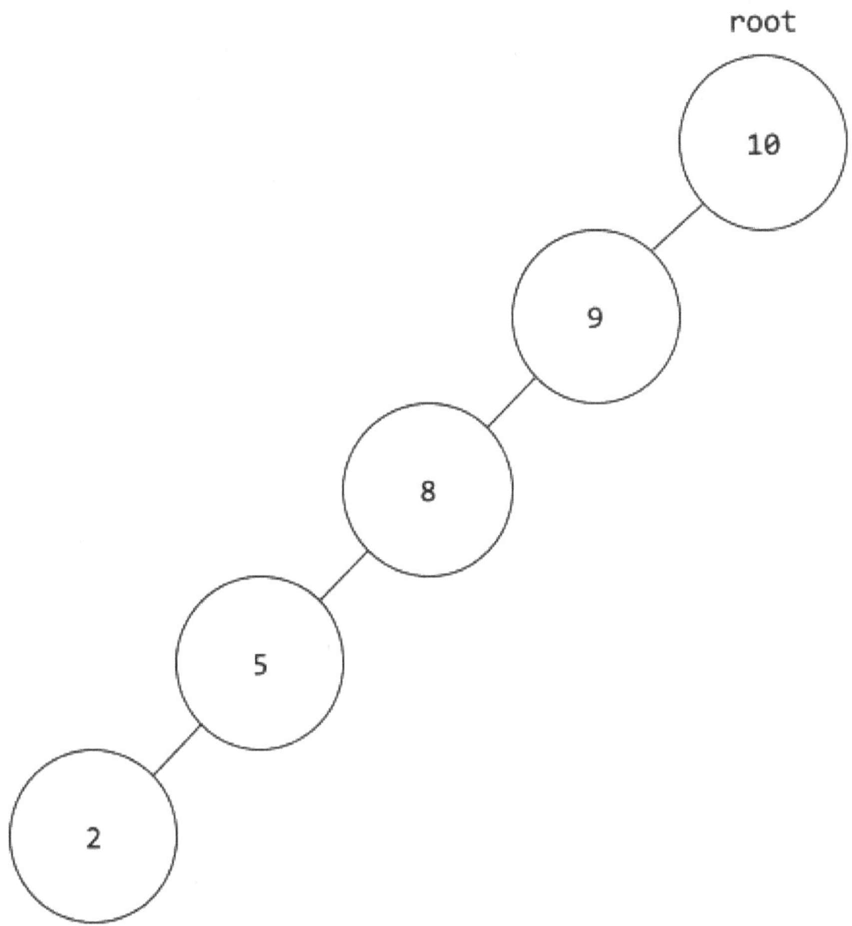

Use Cases

Binary Search Trees are useful when you need:

- Efficient Searching: BSTs provide efficient searching for elements, as you can quickly narrow down the search space by comparing values at each node.

- Ordered Data Storage: The properties of BSTs make them valuable when you need to maintain a sorted collection or retrieve elements in sorted order without additional sorting operations.
- When you need a collection that contains no duplicate elements, you can use a `java.util.Set`. With this interface, you can choose either a HashSet or TreeSet. A TreeSet is really a BST under the hood.

Chapter Summary

In this chapter, we learned about Binary Search Trees (BSTs), which are hierarchical data structures where each node has at most two children, one on the left and one on the right. They are used for organizing data in a way that allows for efficient searching, insertion, and deletion operations.

The most important property of a Binary Search Tree is that for any given node, all nodes in its left subtree have values smaller than it, and all nodes in its right subtree have values greater than it.

You can add a node to a BST in O(log n) time. Removing a node from a BST also takes O(log n) time. Likewise, searching for an element in a Binary Search Tree takes O(log n) time.

Traversing a Binary Search Tree is O(n) and can be done using breadth-first traversal (level-order) or depth-first traversal.

When balanced, BSTs have O(log n) operations. When unbalanced, they can degrade into a linked-list structure if unbalanced, resulting in O(n) time complexity for operations.

Chapter 8
Sorting Algorithms

Have you ever encountered situations where you had a list of items that you wanted to arrange in a specific order, say from smallest to largest? For example, suppose you wanted to sort a list of people according to their age from youngest to oldest, or their height from shortest to tallest. There are many different ways to sort a list of items. In this chapter, we'll cover some popular sorting algorithms. We'll begin with some slow ones and then cover two fast ones.

Selection Sort and Bubble Sort

We already covered these in Chapter 1. Recall the following code:

```java
public class SelectionSort {
    public static void selectionSort(int[] arr) {
        if(arr == null || arr.length < 2)
            return;

        int n = arr.length;
        for(int i = 0; i < n - 1; i++) {
            // Find the minimum element in the
unsorted part of the array
            int minIndex = i;
```

```java
        for(int j = i + 1; j < n; j++) {
            if(arr[j] < arr[minIndex])
                minIndex = j;
        }
        // Swap the minimum element with the
first element in the unsorted part of the array
        int temp = arr[i];
        arr[i] = arr[minIndex];
        arr[minIndex] = temp;
    }
  }
}


public class BubbleSort {
    public static void bubbleSort(int[] arr) {
        if(arr == null || arr.length < 2)
            return;

        int n = arr.length;
        for(int i = 0; i < n - 1; i++) {
            for(int j = 0; j < n - i - 1; j++) {
                // If the current element is greater
than the next element, then swap them
                if(arr[j] > arr[j + 1]) {
                    int temp = arr[j];
                    // Imitates the highest element
bubbling up to the top
                    arr[j] = arr[j + 1];
                    arr[j + 1] = temp;
                }
            }
        }
    }
}
```

Again, since there is an inner loop and an outer loop and both go through the entire array, both algorithms will be $O(n^2)$.

Bubble sort and selection sort are very basic sorting algorithms, which is why they are very slow. We will now take a look at two sorting algorithms that have time complexities that are better than $O(n^2)$ and are therefore faster.

MergeSort

MergeSort is a divide-and-conquer algorithm that recursively divides the input array into two halves, sorts each half, and then merges them back into a single sorted array. Thus, the divide part is the splitting of the array into halves, and the conquer is the merging.

Suppose you want to sort the following array:

99	44	27	5	377	31

We take the array and repeatedly (through recursion) divide into halves:

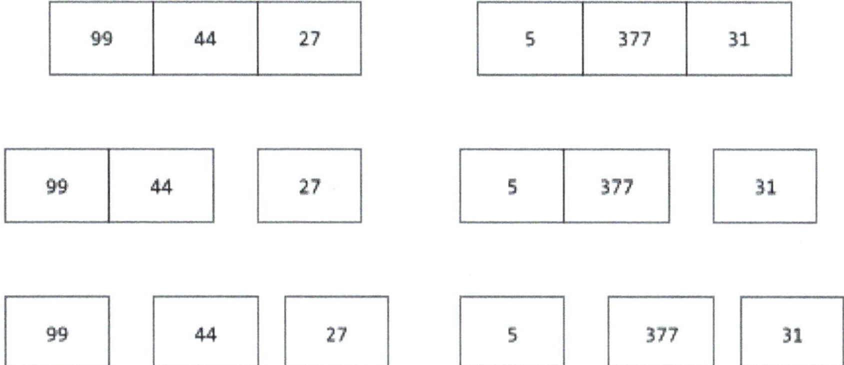

Then we merge:

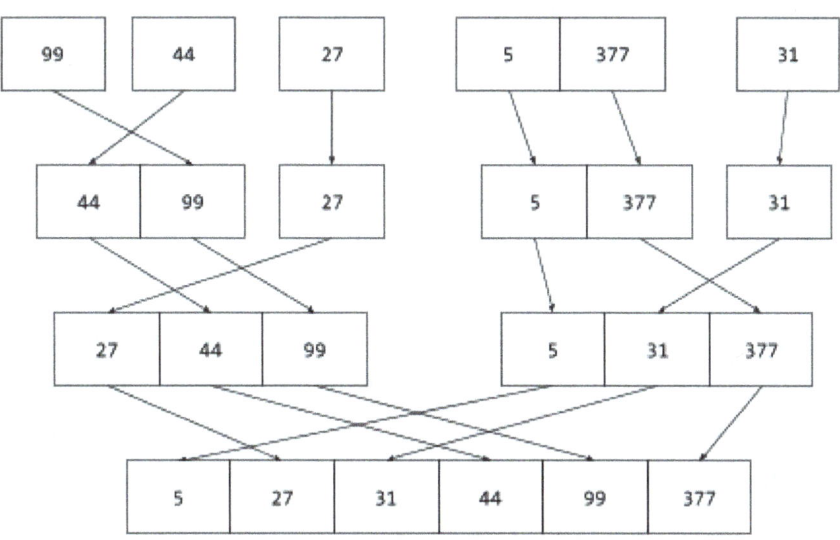

Now, it's time for the code. Let's begin with the method.

```java
public static void mergeSort(int[] arr) {
    int n = arr.length;
    int[] temp = new int[n];
    mergeSortHelper(arr, 0, n - 1, temp);
```

```
}
```

The `mergeSort` method is the entry point for the algorithm. It creates a secondary, temporary array and calls the helper function `mergeSortHelper` to start the recursive sorting process. The temporary array will be used during the merge process.

Second, `mergeSortHelper` will be our recursive method, and its purpose is to divide the input array (and subarrays). The method takes in the array as a parameter, as well as the start and ending index (inclusive) of the subarray with which you want to sort. From the code above, we pass in the entire array as the subarray (i.e., index 0 to n – 1).
The `mergeSortHelper` method will then divide the array in halves into smaller and smaller sections.

First, we need to check if the subarray contains more than one element. If it contains one element, i.e. left = right, then that subarray is already sorted and we can exit out of the method:

```java
private static void mergeSortHelper(int[] arr, int
left, int right, int[] temp) {
    if(left < right) {


    }
}
```

Then we need to divide the subarray into halves. First
we need to find the middle index:

```java
int mid = (right + left) / 2;
```

With that, we can now recursively call `mergeSortHelper`
on the halves. Note that we will use `mid` as the right
bound for the left side, and `mid + 1` as the left bound for
the right side.

```java
// Sort the left half
mergeSortHelper(arr, left, mid, temp);

// Sort the right half
mergeSortHelper(arr, mid + 1, right, temp);
```

The last thing we need to do is merge the two halves
together to make a sorted whole:

```java
// Merge the two sorted halves
merge(arr, left, mid, right, temp);
```

You may have noticed that all we have been doing is just
subdividing the array into subarrays but we haven't
been doing any sorting at all. This is where the `merge`
method comes in.

The `merge` method is going to act like a zipper by taking
two sorted parts of the array and zipping them back
together into the temporary array.

It will take five parameters: the original array (`arr`), the left bound of the left half (`left`), the middle index (`mid`), the right bound of the right half (`right`), and the temporary array (`temp`).

```java
private static void merge(int[] arr, int left, int mid, int right, int[] temp) {

}
```

Recall that the left half of the array is from index `left` to `mid`, and the right half is from index `mid + 1` to `right`.

Because of this, we will use three pointers to keep track of the merging process:
- `i`, which points to the current position in the sorted left half (starting from index `left`).
- `j` points to the current position in the sorted right half (starting from index `mid + 1`).
- `k` points to the current position in the temporary array (starting from index `left`).

With these 3 pointers, here is what we will do:

We will be iterating over the array and comparing the elements at index i and j. Whichever is smaller deserves to go first, so we will add that element to the temporary array. Then, we will increment the respective pointer

(but not the other pointer) and keep comparing values.
This is how it looks like implemented:

```
int i = left;
int j = mid + 1;
int k = left;

while(i <= mid && j <= right) {
    if(arr[i] <= arr[j]) {
        temp[k] = arr[i];
        i++;
    } else {
        temp[k] = arr[j];
        j++;
    }

    k++;
}
```

Eventually, when one of the subarrays is exhausted,
then we know that the other subarray is all greater, as
well as that it's all sorted, so we should add those to the
temp array as well.

```
while(i <= mid) {
    temp[k] = arr[i];
    i++;
    k++;
}

while(j <= right) {
    temp[k] = arr[j];
```

```
        j++;
        k++;
    }
}
```

So, after all that code, we have combined the two
sorted subarrays together and zipped the elements up
in their proper orders in the temporary array. The final
step, obviously, is to copy the temporary array back into
the original array:

```
for(k = left; k <= right; k++)
    arr[k] = temp[k];
```

This step is necessary since the other recursive method
calls rely on the subarray to be sorted, so we can't just
leave the sorted elements in temp.

Here is the code in full:

```
public static void mergeSort(int[] arr) {
    int n = arr.length;
    int[] temp = new int[n];
    mergeSortHelper(arr, 0, n - 1, temp);
}

private static void mergeSortHelper(int[] arr, int
left, int right, int[] temp) {
    if(left < right) {
        int mid = (right + left) / 2;

        // Sort the left half
```

```java
        mergeSortHelper(arr, left, mid, temp);

        // Sort the right half
        mergeSortHelper(arr, mid + 1, right, temp);

        // Merge the two sorted halves
        merge(arr, left, mid, right, temp);
    }
}

private static void merge(int[] arr, int left, int
mid, int right, int[] temp) {
    int i = left;
    int j = mid + 1;
    int k = left;

    while(i <= mid && j <= right) {
        if(arr[i] <= arr[j]) {
            temp[k] = arr[i];
            i++;
        } else {
            temp[k] = arr[j];
            j++;
        }
        k++;
    }

    while(i <= mid) {
        temp[k] = arr[i];
        i++;
        k++;
    }

    while(j <= right) {
```

```
        temp[k] = arr[j];
        j++;
        k++;
    }

    for(k = left; k <= right; k++)
        arr[k] = temp[k];
}
```

Here is a step-by-step explanation of the merge process with an example to help you visualize it:

Suppose you have the following two sorted subarrays: `{-2, -1, 8, 9, 11}` and `{0, 1, 2, 3, 4}`

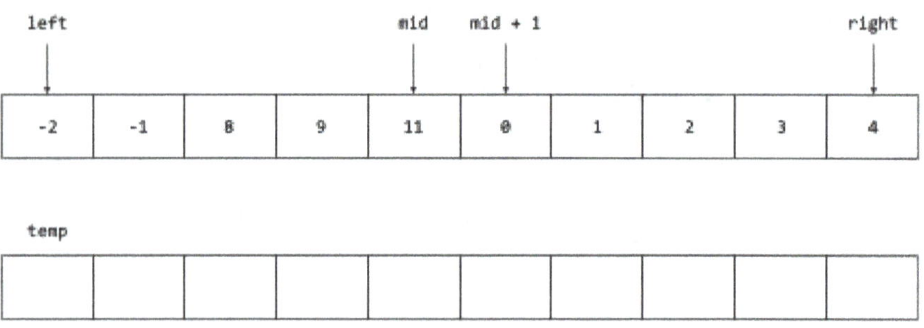

First let's initialize our 3 pointers—i, which will be the same as `left`, j, which will start at `mid + 1`, and k, which will be the same as `left` but in the `temp` array.

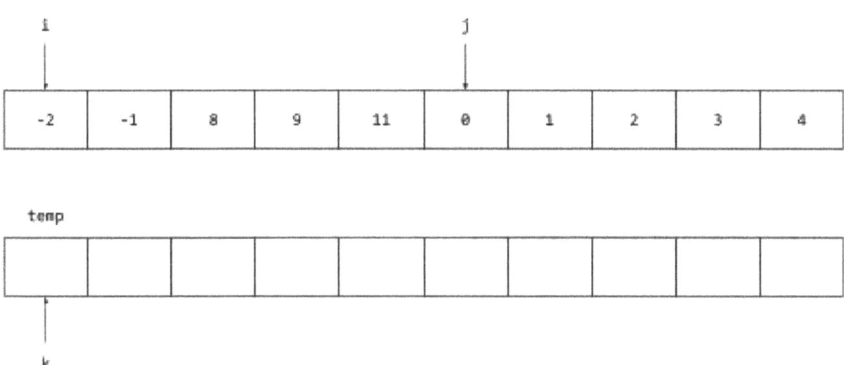

Now we can start our loop. First, comparing `arr[i]` and `arr[j]`, we see that `-2 < 0`, so we copy `-2` into `temp`:

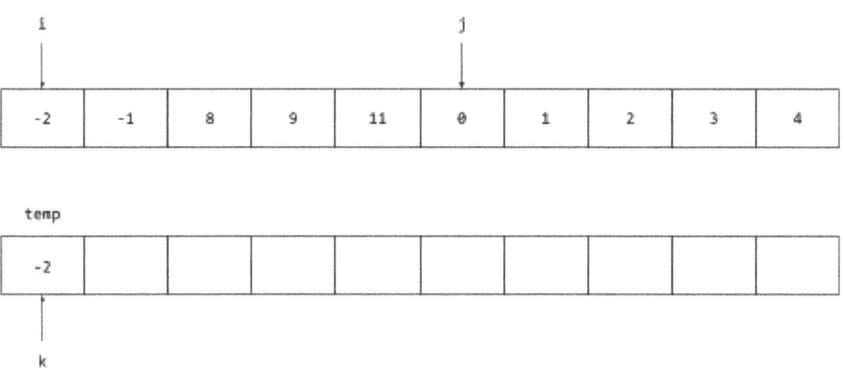

Then we need to increment `i` and `k`.

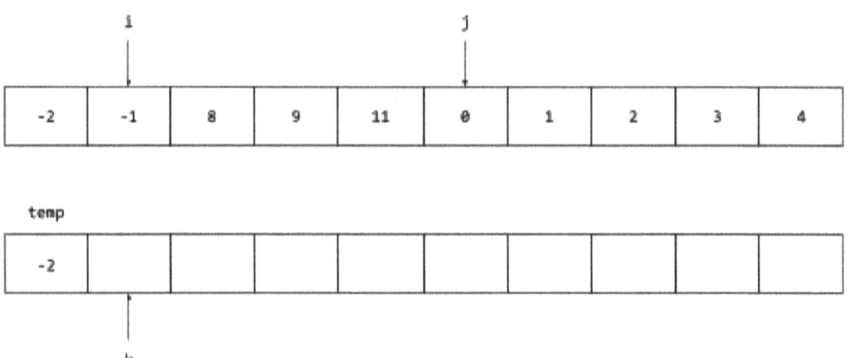

i
j
-2
-1
8
9
11
0
1
2
3
4
temp
-2
k

Again, we compare the two elements, and copy the smaller one into the `temp` array:

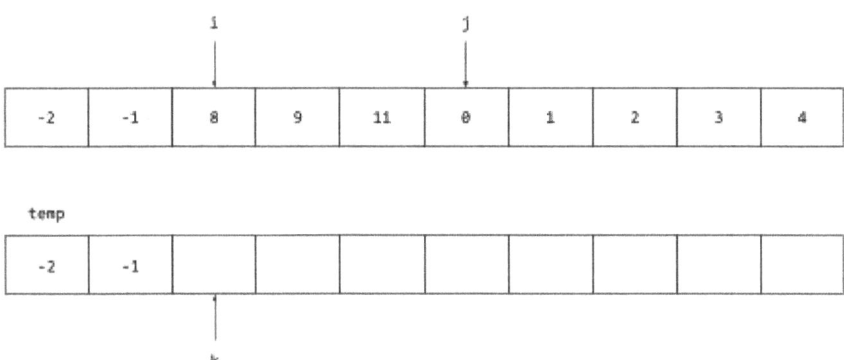

Now we can see that `arr[j]` is smaller than `arr[i]`, so we need to copy that element instead.

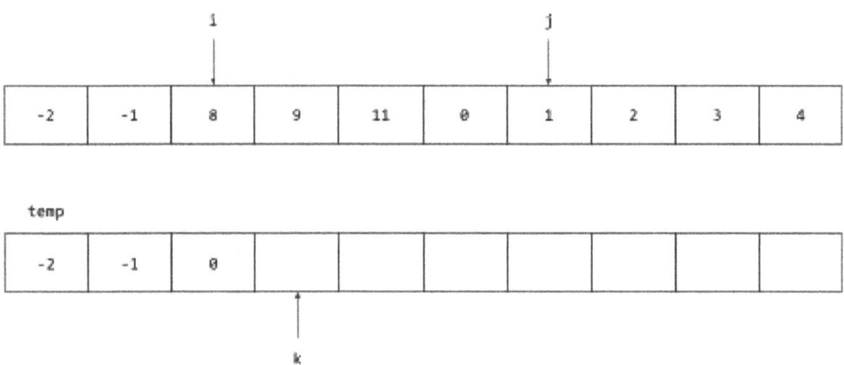

And it continues on like this:

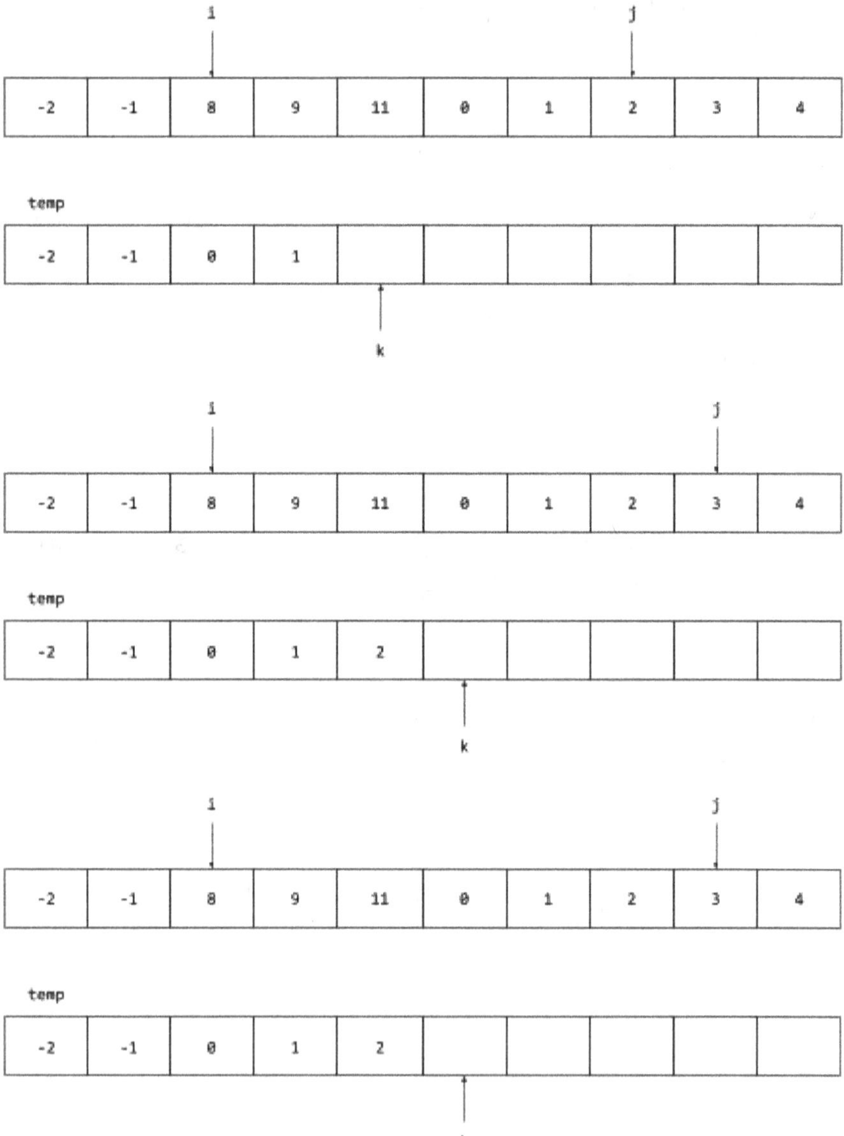

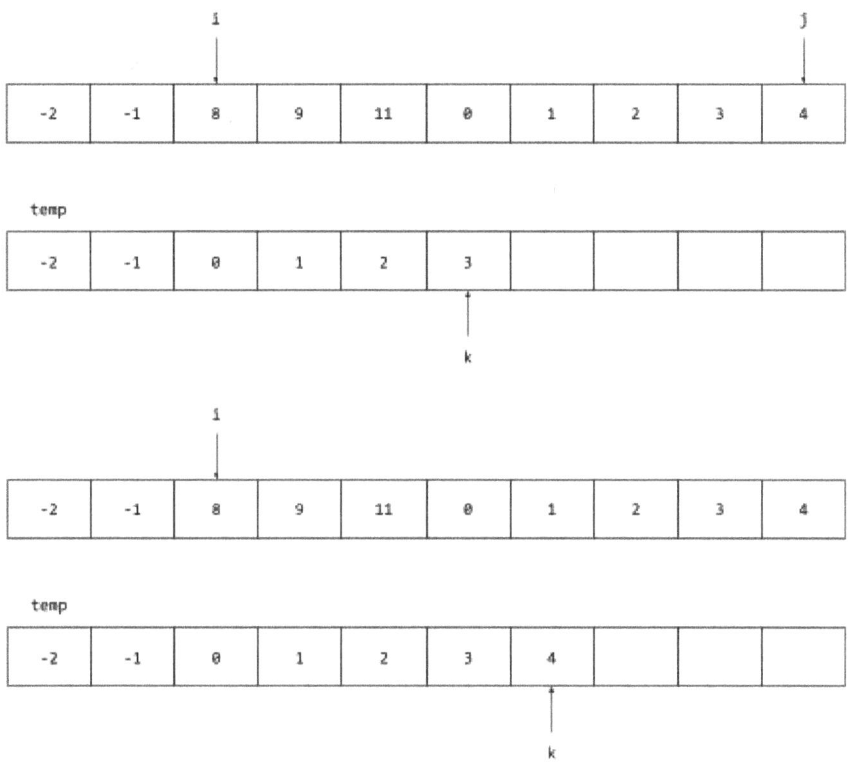

We have reached the end of the right subarray but have not yet exhausted the left. This is when we enter the second loop to copy the rest of the subarray into `temp`:

Now `temp` is sorted and all that is left is to copy it back into `arr`:

arr

-2	-1	0	1	2	3	4	8	9	11

temp

-2	-1	0	1	2	3	4	8	9	11

MergeSort's time complexity is O(n * log n). This is why:

Divide: The array is repeatedly divided into halves until each segment contains only one element. This process takes O(log n) time because we are dividing the array in half at each step, similar to a binary search algorithm.

Merge: After the array is divided into individual elements, the merge operation combines the segments back together while sorting them. This process takes O(n) time because every element in the array is involved in the merging process.

Also note that every Divide step, i.e. a call to `mergeSortHelper`, also results in a call to the `merge` step. This means that every divide step entails a merge step and that means that the overall time complexity is O(divide) * O(merge), or O(n) * O(log n) = O(n log n)

MergeSort's time complexity of O(n log n) makes it a much more efficient sorting algorithm compared to Bubble Sort and Selection Sort, both of which have a time complexity of $O(n^2)$, since n log n is less than n^2.

The final sorting algorithm is presented here called QuickSort. As the name implies, it is a very fast and efficient way to sort elements. Since it does not require an additional temporary array like merge sort does, it is more space-efficient.

QuickSort

Like with our MergeSort algorithm, our QuickSort method will recursively subdivide our array into halves, stopping when we get to the subarrays with lengths 1 or 0. Let's start with the same entry point as before:

```java
public class QuickSort {
    public static void quickSort(int[] arr) {
        partition(arr, 0, arr.length - 1);
    }

    private static void partition(int[] arr, int lo,
int hi) {

    }
}
```

Three things have changed: 1) There is no more temporary array. 2) The `left` and `right` variables have been renamed to `lo` and `hi`. This is purely personal preference, so you can change this back if you wanted to. 3) The helper method has been renamed to `partition`, since we will be partitioning elements as you will soon see.

Now let's implement the base case—if `lo` and `hi` are equal or `lo` is greater than `hi`, the subarray is invalid, so we can exit out of the method:

```
if(lo >= hi)
    return;
```

Now we can get into the meat of the method.

QuickSort works by going through the following steps:
1. Select an element, called a "pivot", which we will use to rearrange the rest of the array. For this implementation we will choose `pivot` to be the middle element, between `lo` and `hi`. This step is called "partitioning" since we will use `pivot` as the partition between the smaller elements on the left, and the bigger elements on the right.
2. Start with a pointer `i` at `lo` and a pointer `j` at `hi`.
3. Keep going forward with `i` until you find an element out of place, which means go forward until you find an element that is greater than

`pivot` (only elements less than `pivot` should be to its left).

4. Likewise, go backwards with `j` until you find an element less than `pivot`.
5. Now that you have two elements out of place in both `i` and `j`, swap those two variables
6. Repeat from step 3 until `i` and `j` have crossed.

Before continuing on with the algorithm let's implement this first.

Step 1: Choose a pivot

```
int mid = (lo + hi) / 2;
int pivot = arr[mid];
```

Step 2: Initialize i and j

```
int i = lo;
int j = hi;
```

Steps 3-4: Loop until i and j cross, going forward with i and backward with j:

```
while(i <= j) {
    while(arr[i] < pivot)
        i++;

    while(arr[j] > pivot)
        j--;
}
```

Step 5: Swap and move forward with i and j:

```
if(i <= j) {
    int temp = arr[i];
    arr[i] = arr[j];
    arr[j] = temp;

    i++;
    j--;
}
```

Step 6: Repeat until `i` and `j` have crossed. This is already taken care of in the `while` loop.

Now we can proceed with our algorithm:
7. Check if the left subarray needs to be sorted. At the end of the loop, j will have crossed over i, meaning j will be on the left side of pivot while i will be on the right. Thus, the left subarray will consist of elements from `lo` up to j. If a subarray does indeed exist here, i.e. `lo < j`, then call `quickSort` again on this subarray.
8. Likewise, do the same thing for the subarray from i up to `hi`.

```java
if(lo < j)
    partition(arr, lo, j);

if(i < hi)
    partition(arr, i, hi);
```

And that's it! Our QuickSort algorithm has been fully implemented. Here is the code in full:

```java
public class QuickSort {
    public static void quickSort(int[] arr) {
        partition(arr, 0, arr.length - 1);
    }

    private static void partition(int[] arr, int lo,
```

```java
int hi) {
    if(lo >= hi)
        return;

    int mid = (lo + hi) / 2;
    int pivot = arr[mid];

    int i = lo;
    int j = hi;

    while(i <= j) {
        while(arr[i] < pivot)
            i++;

        while(arr[j] > pivot)
            j--;

        if(i <= j) {
            int temp = arr[i];
            arr[i] = arr[j];
            arr[j] = temp;

            i++;
            j--;
        }
    }

    if(lo < j)
        partition(arr, lo, j);

    if(i < hi)
        partition(arr, i, hi);
}
}
```

If that didn't make sense to you, we can demonstrate with an example. Start with the following unsorted array:

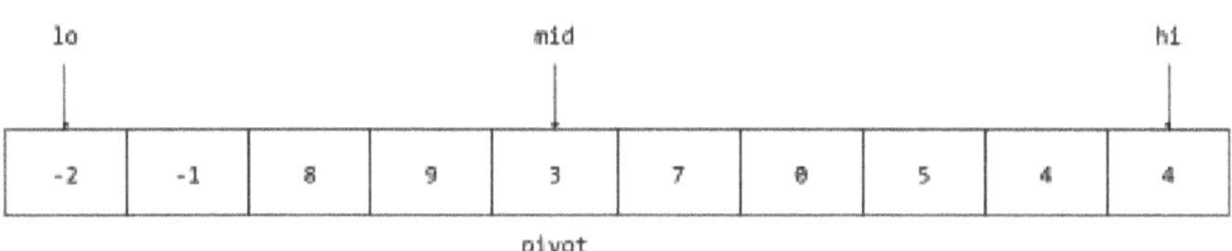

Our goal, as we stated before, is to use `pivot` as our partition. All elements smaller than `pivot` will go on the left, and all elements greater will go on the right. First, we loop with `i` and `j` until we find elements that are out of place:

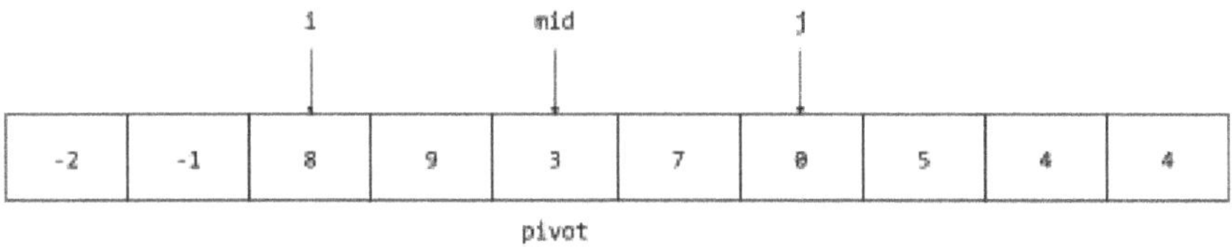

Then we swap them and advance both:

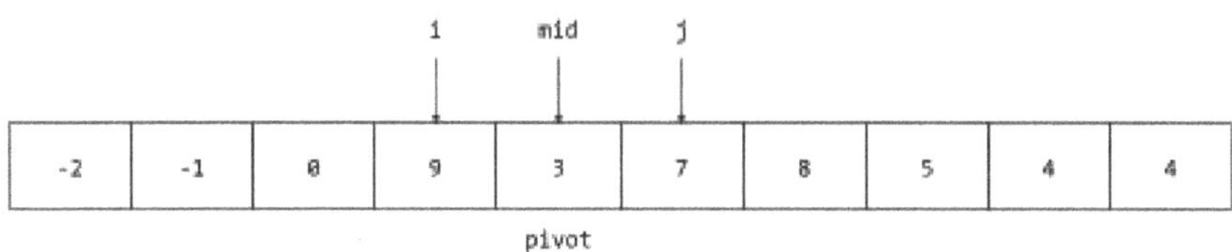

Again we loop with `i` and `j`:

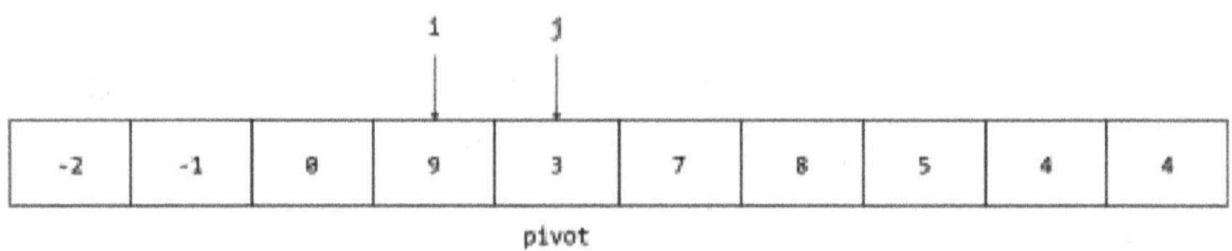

We swap, advance, and stop here because they have crossed.

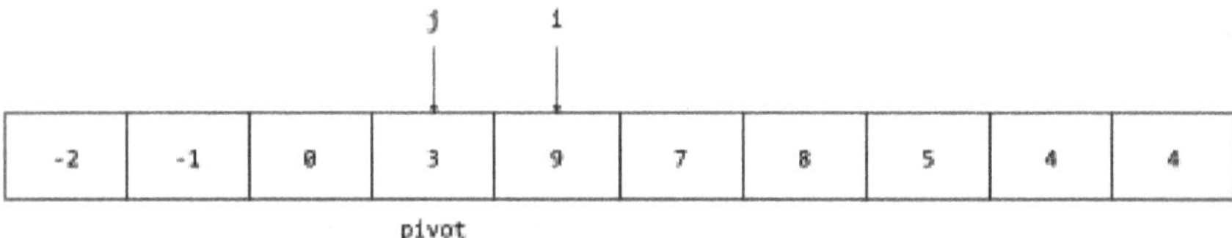

Now you can see that all elements to the left of the pivot are less than it, and all elements to the right of the pivot are greater than it.

Let's keep going. Since here the QuickSort separates into two recursive method calls, we'll only analyze the left subarray from `lo` to `j`, but the right subarray will be sorted in the same way.

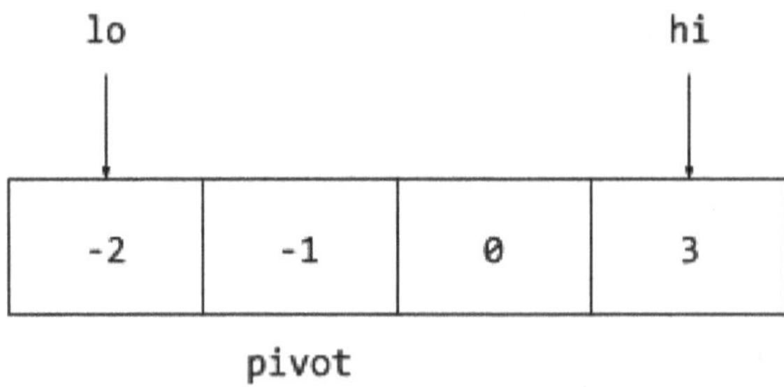

Looping again with `i` and `j` until we find elements that are out of place, we end up with this:

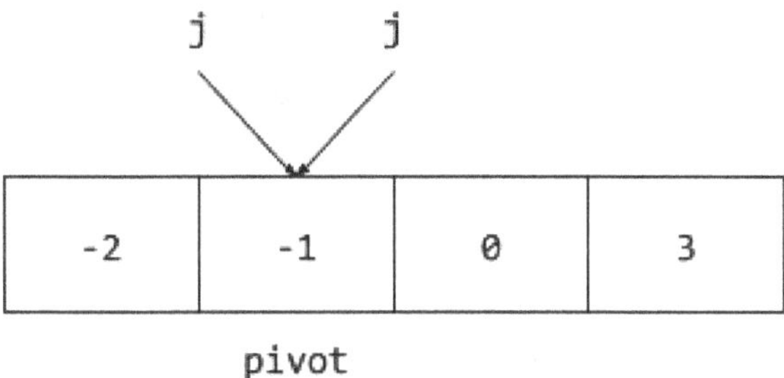

We can stop here and see that this subarray is already sorted. If you want, you can go ahead and try the algorithm on the right subarray that we left above and you can see that it works.

The QuickSort algorithm is similar to MergeSort in that its average-case time complexity is O(n log n). For each divide step, there is also the step that sorts the elements around the pivot, meaning that the time complexity is O(n) * O(log n), or O(n log n).

Unfortunately, QuickSort can be $O(n^2)$ in the worst case. Suppose you get an array that's already sorted and you take the leftmost element to be the pivot:

With the pivot at the front, we have n - 1 elements to partition.

Then, the next recursive quicksort step is to partition n - 2 elements:

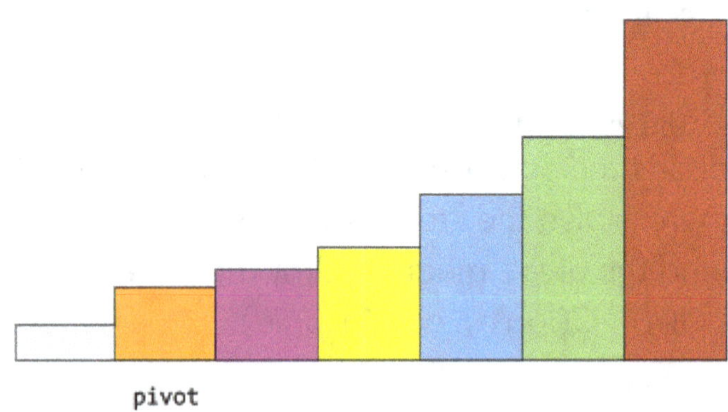

And next with n – 3 elements to partition:

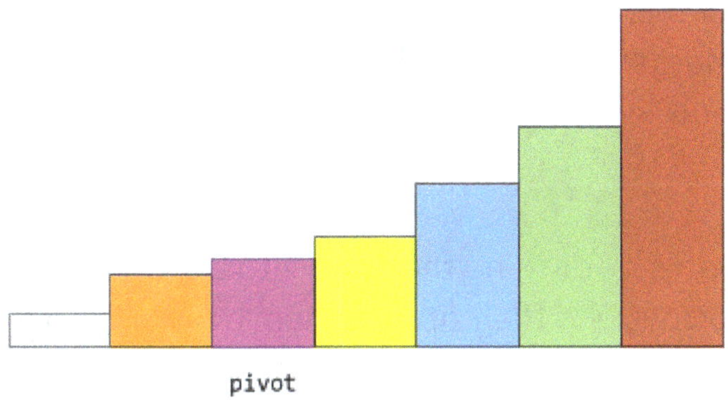

As you can see, this is similar to our quadratic sorts earlier. The number of elements that we have to partition only decrements each time in the recursive call. Essentially the time complexity becomes:

$$(n - 1) + (n - 2) + \ldots + 1 = \frac{n(n-1)}{2} = \frac{1}{2}(n^2 - n)$$

Thus, the worst-case time for QuickSort is $O(n^2)$. That's why it's very important to choose the correct pivot.

The good news about QuickSort, though, is its average and best time complexities are $O(n \log n)$, which are similar to MergeSort. Plus, QuickSort uses less memory because it does not require an additional temporary array.

Chapter Summary

In this chapter, we learned about two more sorting algorithms: MergeSort and QuickSort. Both use recursive divide-and-conquer methods to sort the subarrays.

MergeSort works by dividing the array into small 1- or 2-element subarrays and then zipping them back up into a sorted temporary array and copying that back into the original array.

QuickSort, on the other hand, picks pivots from the array, partitions elements around the pivot, and then after that sorts the left and right subarrays.

MergeSort is always O(n log n), but it requires an extra array of space. QuickSort is usually O(n log n) but if it is implemented poorly, it can be $O(n^2)$. However, it requires no extra space.